EC(O)LOGUES

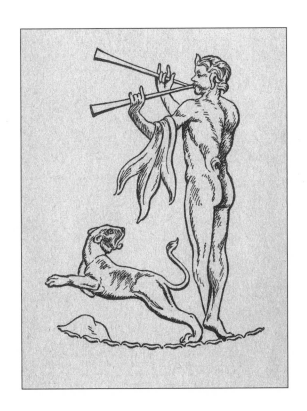

EC(O)LOGUES

PETER LAMBORN WILSON

Station Hill
of Barrytown

Published by Station Hill Press, Inc., 120 Station Hill Road, Barrytown, NY 12507, as a project of the Institute for Publishing Arts, Inc., in Barrytown, New York, a not-for-profit, tax-exempt organization [501(c)(3)], supported in part by grants from the New York State Council on the Arts, a state agency.

Online catalogue: www.stationhill.org

e-mail: publishers@stationhill.org

Interior and cover design by Susan Quasha.

Cover Image: Philip Taaffe, *Passage* (2009), mixed media on paper, 10 1/2 × 12 inches, Private collection, Courtesy Gagosian Gallery. Copyright 2009 Phillip Taaffe, all rights reserved.

Library of Congress Cataloging-in-Publication Data

Wilson, Peter Lamborn.
  Ec(o)logues / Peter Lamborn Wilson.
    p. cm.
A Menippean satire (mixed poetry and prose) inspired by Virgil's Eclogues.
ISBN 978-1-58177-115-2 (alk. paper)
I. Title. II. Title: Ecologues.
PR6073.I4736E36 2010
821'.914—dc22

                    2009041815

Manufactured in the United States of America

Thanx & tips-o-the-fez to:

Anne Waldman, Stacy Szymaszek & the St Mark's Poetry Project; Judith Malina, The Living Theater & the LBC Anarchist Forum; Raymond Foye, Philip Taaffe, Bill Breeze, Shiv Mirabito, Jake Rabinowitz, James Irsay, Charles and Hélène Potter, Jim Fleming, Jack Collom, Mick Taussig, Gordon Campbell, Robert Kelly, Michael Brownstein, Phong Bui, Roger Van Voorhees, the *Brooklyn Rail,* Joel Kovel and Karen Charman (*Capitalism Nature Socialism* 20/3, Sept. 09); Chuck Stein, George and Susan Quasha, Jenny Fox, Alana Siegel and Sam Truitt.

CONTENTS

FOREWORD BY CHARLES STEIN   ix

Shepherds' Calendar   3

Green Orpheus   15

Endarkenment   19

Pantisocratic Idyll   21

Murphy's Eclogue   23

Ginsberg Gilgamesh   26

Ten Golden Apples   27

Comix Eclogue   32

Eclogue for Hekate   34

Brook Farm Eclogue   41

Neo-Pastoralist Manifesto   42

Neo-Pastoralist Diet Plan   46

FLORA   49

Hiber-Nation   52

New Jersey Eclogue   54

Blake/Saturn/Palmer   56

Pastoral Prose   72

Herm   82

Pastoral Roadkill   86

Benares Eclogue   87

Animus/Anima/Animal   90

Anglo-Irish Big House Eclogue   93

The Jukes Eclogue   98

Goat Prose   103

Pastoral Pigeons   105

Equites   106

AgitProp   107

Violence Prose 110

SPORES 117

Mud Season 125

Corn Eclogue 134

Negative Capability Eclogue 139

The ROUT 142

LIST OF ILLUSTRATIONS

"Piper & Dog", from *Virgil: The Pastoral Poems: The Text of the Eclogues with a Translation* by E. V. Rieu (London: Penguin, 1967).   Half-title page

"Eros", from Bernard de Montfaucon, *L'Antiquité expliquée* (Paris, 1719), in Robert Calasso, *The Marriage of Cadmus and Harmony* (New York: Vintage, 1994).   16

"FLORA attired by the ELEMENTS", by Henry Fuseli, in Erasmus Darwin, *The Botanic Garden: A Poem in Two Parts* (London, 1791; Scolar Press facsimile, London, 1973)   49

William Blake, "Frontispiece", from *The Illustrations of William Blake for Thornton's Virgil with the First Eclogue and the Imitation by Ambrose Philips*, intro. by Geoffrey Keanes (London, The Nonsuch Press, 1937).   56

Fifteen of the woodcuts from Blake's *Thornton's Virgil*, *ibid.*   57–60

Blake, "Thenot & Colinet", pencil sketch for an unrealized woodcut, *ibid.*   64

"Sani" (the Hindu Saturn); traditional.   65

Three prints by Samuel Palmer, from *Samuel Palmer 1805-1881: Vision and Landscape*, by W. Vaughn *et al.* (London: The British Museum Press, 2005).   68–71

"The Triumph of Priapus", from Francesco Colonna, *Hypnerotomachia Poliphili: The Strife of Love in a Dream*, trans. and intro. by Joscelyn Godwin (orig. ed. Venice, 1499; London: Thames & Hudson, 1999).   144

"Satyr & Youth", from de Montfaucon, *ibid.*   150

Foreword

It is my hope that this book by Peter Lamborn Wilson will come as something of a revelation to the world of poetry: a revelation that poetry this good and good in this way can be produced in our times; good as rhythmically and sonorously exciting, expressive, intuitive, intelligent, well-measured, suitably barbaric, historically redolent, politically, metaphysically, even soteriologically astute. A revelation because we are unaccustomed to poetry that is not predominately ironical in statement, excessively self-reflective in attitude, or committed to the demolition of its own means, that is at once so extraordinarily urbane in spirit and down-home, downright funky in expressive spontaneity, not to mention intellectually complex, with a generous salting of wit and cognitive play. All this, too, without, through naiveté, ignorance, or obtuseness, exposing itself to critical missiles poised like ICBMs to be deployed against work that attempts just what these poems actually achieve.

And I would hazard a reason why: that the stance of the poetry—and Peter Lamborn Wilson has earned his stance through decades of committed prose—that the stance of this poetry, in the complexity of its reflection, the radical specificity of its attentions, and the intensity of its care—is in every breath a *committed* poetry, and committed in a singular, highly individuated, unpredictable way.

The verse may take its cue from Allen Ginsberg and William Blake, but its intellectual purview shows intimacy with Kropotkin, Proudhon, Engels, Swedenborg, Paracelsus, Agrippa, Erasmus Darwin, Pierre Clastres, Henry Corbin, Charles Fourier, and many others of an equally august if unconventionally referenced notoriety.

Wilson weaves a visionary poetics through an explicit politics, an explicit politics through an exuberant sense of imaginative freedom. Wilson names his political and spiritual agenda "neo-pastoralism" and mines the pastoral tradition of the venerable ancients—Theocritus, Virgil, Edmund Spencer—for material that reprises and expands themes from his previous pronunciamentos: *Green Hermeticism, Escape from the Nineteenth*

Century," "The Shamanic Trace," Pirate Utopias, The Temporary Autonomous Zone, to name but a few of his titles.

The poetry is moderated by prose interludes in a variety of genres that develop thoughts in a manner appropriate to the energy of the poetry, not so much by providing conceptual bases for its contents (in a way it does that too), but by the sheer aptness of contiguity and multiplicitous resonance, worked out and placed with an intelligence whose lucidity is as disruptive as the rampant audacity of the verse.

A persistent organizing theme is the hypothesis (due to the late Pierre Clastres) that the historical arrival of "civilization" with its literacy, collectively organized agriculture, division of labor into rulers, administrators, and drones, its authoritarian religion, private property, and massive armies—in short, the advent of The State—came about through the failure of precise social formations that for tens of thousands of years had functioned to ward off and dissipate the agglomeration and centralization of political power. Modern humanity (since 4000 BCE) has invented its own ignorance of the deep human past—and called only what superceded and suppressed it—History. Wilson sets off in search of the traces of social practices now long eclipsed and finds them cannily in the most unlikely places.

The metaphysical posture is pantheism or "pagan monotheism," aligned with anarchism. The work: to conjure an aggressive pantheism through a veil, haze, or prism of pastoral idealism—the lure of nature realized through the dangerous, bottom-feeding numinosity demonstrably intrinsic to it.

Orthodox (Abrahamic) monotheists routinely slander pantheism, averring that it entails, in practice, a slothful relaxation of the spirit and a general abnegation of conscience: if God is All, what need for moral discipline, intellectual rigor, or the restraint of native delinquency?

But if moral rigor as practiced until now proves to be the absolute repression of the divine in the world and the vassal of Statist discipline, even relaxation and license become tactics for the recovery of natural and divine values. It turns out, however, as any reader of *Ec(o)logues* may very well attest, that the attentions and affirmations demanded by pantheist-anarchism may prove anything but easily achieved. The affirmation of everything will test the stomach of any of us. It is the discipline and conscience of such an ontological perspective and the transgressive sacrality it entails, that there, where one cannot imagine the sacred, is precisely where one's practice must seek it out. In that sense *Ec(o)logues* is itself spiritual praxis, for reader and poet alike.

CHARLES STEIN
February, 2010
Barrytown, New York

EC(O)LOGUES

Shepherds' Calendar

January

Bumpkinism
                paganus: literally
                                shit kicking hick
unlike urbane monotheists who know
that Nature has been defined by the
Nature Police as that which is not
unnatural.
                   No lurching around the Maypole
                             of Merry Mount
                                      abusing the sacraments
No priapaean pricksongs or
                   sub-Jungian nitrate fertilizers for
the rosin clear air of Antiquity
                   laced with sighs and secretions.
No fecundating the wiccan furrows.

February

the anodyne pastoral of
                  funeral mutes.
All Corn All The Time.
                          Exiled to Appalachia
now rivals for the hand
of fair So-&-So.
                  In the hayloft.
Behind the barn.
                    Behind the privy.
Sell the farm to a developer
                                move
to Necropolis, Florida
land of pyramids & terminal
                air-conditioning.

March

Emerson's Gaseous
                    Invertebrate

a New Grange for the
                    rural strange.

Veneration of Nature without fear
is nothing but sentimental Bambiism

                    suffocated stars.

Re-enchantment of the landscape means
                    literally re-enchant

                              telluric mycoremediation
possibly animal sacrifice

                    even omophagy.

April

Pastoral Letter
        from Bishop
                Lamborn Bey
                        to flock
crozier in one hand
                vaudeville hook or crook
poised to bless
                    quite empty.
The sheep look up
        the sheep are free to vote
                glatt kosher or
                halal
kleftikon the roast mutton of kleptomaniacs
in hock to the corpse of April. In
carne asada. Spiritual cannibalism.
Every supper might be yr last.
                  Barbacoa
pirate salmagundi salt pork stewed in
pepper & gunpowder—
             Flambé.
And the Church itself a Spanish galleon
sunk in fathoms of starfish & doubloons.

May

Desire itself is a form of gravy

                              a Midwestern ghazal.

Cheese is the food of love.
Salt licks & lightning rods—lingams
of the Driftless Region.

                           The lazy yokel

plows a crooked furrow:
UFOs—radionics—lost Effigy Mounds
concrete gardens—junkyard spaceships
surrounded by corn.

Lying on midnight hillside surrounded by cows
waiting for meteor showers
the color of wormwood

                            —moonflowers

blooming by the old hotel.

June

mildewed screened-in log
                              little idylls
insinuations of pines & hemlocks
                              shshshhh
                              pssst
frogs barn-owls locusts sylphs
                              of the Air
weekend Taoism is better than
                              none at all.

July

Our favorite eclogue rains all day
cloaking verdure in hexes of cold mist
shepherds & shepherdettes huddle in huts
brew tea on spirit lamps—

                                avicennan effusions.

Increasingly sacred & therefore

                                  monotonous rain's

pluviomantic pineal cold blue nose
grows canine buds & decodes
whispering pines' aromal hieroglyphs.

August

Somewhere in Delaware County maybe
failing dairy farm not far from Delhi
the unknown Green Messiah is now
out behind the barn jerking off like
                              Rimbaud
like Hylas locked in the privy with an old
                    Myths of Greece & Rome
illustrated with naked engravings.
                        The Gaian Savior
skinnydipping in an irrigation ditch
pisses underwater.
                    The HooDoo Redeemer
drops bib overalls in the little copse
                              of poplars
rhododendrons blackberries on the
far side of the pasture & its bourgeois
                                    cows
a tulip sized priapus worshipped by no one
but the sad sylph of the glade
spills his miraculous seed on the
                        corpse of Pan.

September

Ichabod Crane: narrative ego or Ich
epiphanizes landscape as banquet
each pumpkin a pie to his
                              allegorical eye
beneath the sigillum of a Dutch
                              Blondie
crowned with Persephone's poppies.
The heedless horseman then becomes Pluto
& Crane the failed Eleusinian initiate
come 1000 years too late—
                              belated—
already nostalgic for a present
always slipping out of his grasp
like a greased pig in a graveyard
heavy garden of puffballs morels
              & pushy mushrooms.

October

French aristo's wanted to be milkmaids
the way boyscouts want to be Indians
piling artifice upon artificiality
                              down on the farm
one lax hayloft day amongst the
                           shiftless hip-billies
honeysuckle tangled privy really
twangs yr lyre.
                      Noses notice
most of our food not only ends but
                       begins in shit.
Crops adore Ovidian perversions—
Harvest of pistils & pizzles & wombs
                    of honey.

November

Trashy Bacchus gets into intestines
like Jesus in the bread.

Lonesome farmboys.

Theology of things as usual.

Full Irish breakfast.

Wages Are Death.

December

Suburban eclogue: Meanwhile Omar
& Hafez are making a little extra income
selling garden fruit which is also
the body of G-d.

                And why not?
In real life anti-pastoral forces
have already triumphed. Luckily
this is not exactly real life.
A greener meaner Jesus to lead us
into Endarkenment—

                out of
the dank realm of Herod
            the Machine.

Green Orpheus

Alone at the Pond—
was Thoreau queer? his relation
to nature secretly Theocrito-Virgilian just
where he valued it for
                              itself alone
& not as some woman to be
                    conquered & plowed?
All pastoral is queer
au naturel onanism en plein air
with visualization exercizes from
                              Coleridge
                              Rimbaud
                              Crowley
faun as faun   undine as undine
                              nymph as nymph
in bee-loud meadows
                    circle jerk with
                         genies of the
                              locus.
Queer for Nature.
Orpheus charms trees & beasts only after
rejecting women for boys.
                         Idylls are idle
cultivations of a vast otium
                         of goat songs
delirious ethnographies
                              Hyacinthus
                              Hylas
                              sterile love
"the unnatural
is also natural" sez Goethe—

orphic artifacts.
Sibylline homoplatonism
queer satori
everything a perfectly adequate
symbol of itself
in a standstill in the afternoon
shade
of a temporary nirvana.

The severed head of Orpheus still singing
washes up on Lesbos island of lesbo's.
Severed heads are queer: Friar Bacon's
                              Brazen Head
                        Bran the Blessed
                          St John the Conqueroo
                          Blueplate Special
Baphomet of the sodomitical Templars
Orpheus
                  torn apart by angry feminists
                          a head full of mana.
                                      Sappho
                                      Hecate
                                      Cybele
                                      Gaia
                                      sterile love
generates progeny in the Unseen World. Just to have an aesthetics of
Nature therefore is already queer in itself—non-fecund—non-repro-
ductive—pure imagination in the dirtiest sense of the Pathetic Fallacy.
Degraded animism. Or, to coin a slogan: No Natural Without the Unnat-
ural—scrawled on a wall with the rune of the Hanged Man. To enchant
animals is to be enchanted into an animal—original goal of all human
mysticism. To become the Totem. Temporary Immortality.

      Every biosphere requires a tasty atmosphere
      of the magical & perverse
                          the anomalous
inwardness of Nature
                  Hecate's moonstruck
                        sterility.
                              Green
Hermes Green Orpheus
                  avataric

H.D. Thoreau
who neither sowed
nor did he reap—
spiritual boyscout of the aesthetic
hermeneutics
of Second Nature, as Marx noted—
"idiocy of rural life."

ENDARKENMENT

Neo-Pastoralism resembles that peasant mob who besiege the castle of
Baron Doktor Ben Franklinstein in the last reel waving scythes & torches
chanting Down With Progress—Ban Electricity. Kulak Exilarchs. Give us
back our lost eleven days. Jacobite Jacobins, toasting the King Over The
Water as mystical collectivity. *Every Man A King*, by Huey Long. Radical
agrarians in a land with no agriculture, baffled & resentful. The Countess
of Pembroke's Arcadia re-designed by JG Ballard to replicate an eternal
shopping mall converting all space Space/Time into

$$\text{Paramus NJ on a}$$
$$\text{slow Monday night}$$

in a CyberWorld chat-room on the

$$\text{outskirts of Sartre's Hell.}$$
$$\text{Spitting out our}$$

serotonin uptake inhibitors

$$\text{easy prey}$$

for colorful conspiracy theories

$$\text{everything that stinks of the police.}$$

Farms always already foreclosed
the bitter pottage of bourgeois self-consciousness.

$$\text{Give us back}$$

our sunk Atlantis our lost Arcadia
where hobo is king & Apollo's cows are
rustled by the world's first pastoralist

$$\text{social bandit baby.}$$

Then Indra rescues the cows &

$$\text{the Monsoon breaks.}$$
$$\text{Snakes}$$

broods of sleepy monsters yearning
to slip into rural sloth

$$\text{doze away}$$

the Late Neolithic

        grew wroth with

vulgar young gods

always making rude noises &

        advocating Progress.

      REVERSION

        without electricity

under the terror of the stars

      ARMED NOSTALGIA

      MUTABILITIE

        in fact

anything to avoid the so-called

        dignity of labor.

Out here we wear the weather

inside our clothes

     sunk in sloth &

        accedia.

PANTISOCRATIC IDYLL

It's true that shepherds simply have
                    more spare time
for poetic contests & trading dozens.
Same root as amoeba—one song
             changes into two—
                  Amoebian verse
—Onan the Barbarian meets monocular
             Polyphemus in a
TV wrestling match or hadith of
            the Hidden Treasure—
Erasmus Darwin's primordial unicellular
animal mundi or Sole Evolver—
              deus patheticus.
There must be at least two shepherds
for transhumance to transpire with grace
to build a bothy for us "both Arcadians."
The Orphic trick consists of a Pythagorean
mutual tuning between centuries of grazing
& the landscape open to slanting light.
Meadows of flesh. Symbiosis with bees.

Coleridge & Southey actually launch their Pantisocracy
in rural Pennsylvania. They compose alternate verses
of a vast *Amoibaion* (2 vol.'s 8vo.
Philadelphia 1794 marbled endpapers gilt &
engravings. Slightly foxed) & are
swept up in the Whiskey Rebellion
its Biblical prophecies & French Revolutionary
                connotations.

Possible scenes: Coleridge scores laudanum
from peripatetic German Paracelsan hex doctor
Coleridge attempts to seduce Southey's wife
visit to Ephrata—conversations with Rosicrucian
Dr Christopher Witt herbalist alchemist &
last living disciple of Johannes Kelpius
young Jonathan Chapman eccentric pomologist
Swedenborgian missionary not yet known as Johnny Appleseed
Coleridge high on tincture of Cannabis Indica
experiences ecstatic communion with Nature
Southey joins Whiskey Rebel militia
in fit of apocalyptic fervor.

                    Pantisocracy Armed.
Arrested by agents of Alexander Hamilton
(the villain). Jail in Philadelphia—
all-night conversation with Rev. Herman Husband
the bearded barefoot preacher who
sparked the uprising like a
                         lithograph
from Blake's *America: A Prophecy.*
Deported back to England broke &
                         disillusioned
they resume their actual historical lives.

See the ghost of Coleridge in Western Pennsylvania
as the Earthly Jerusalem the forks of the Ohio
four rivers flowing out of Eden. Indians
are the Ten Lost Tribes. Orpheus is the Green Messiah
just for a summer. Another America that
                              might have been.
Snake-bitten we return from Hell
with nothing to show for it but this music.

Murphy's Eclogue

(as in Arcimboldo) Winter's fungus lips
look vaguely psychoactive—his ivy hair
mantic & delphic
                              Mick Murphy
late shanachie of Ballinskellig
lived exclusively on Guiness hashish
                              the odd pig's foot
                                        (cubeen)
seemed sometimes to melt into some
squalid rural landscape by Max Ernst
illustrating Flann O'Brien's *Swim Two Birds*
                              or *Poor Mouth*
spoke the purest Erse in Co. Kerry
in the bar of that seasodden Hotel
run by spoiled monks
                              fifty years
of blocked drains spilt beer & bad tobacco
without his teeth looked like Winter himself
a dirty Punch in a dirty mackintosh.
He was never seen out-of-doors & yet
was covered in moss & watercress
                              like Mad Sweeny.
Caesar misheard those Celts he claimed
told him the only thing they feared was
that the sky might fall on them—
                              what they actually said
was that they feared falling into the sky.
A halo of Republican violence hovered over Murphy's
                              stained tweed cap
—once he grew grass for some IRA faction—they were

going to call it "Kerry Gold"—but
                                        the rain killed it.

Snake in a raincoat
his features blurred into Mandelbrot sets of
                                        bad bad tobacco—
magic that's real but never works
or almost never
& its masters all die poor & sad
alone in a rotten-thatched cottage
                                        on the strand
with a thousand empty bottles.

We spent our childhood summer vacations there
playing in the sand between Pirate's Tower
& the Nuns' Sanitarium.

Murphy becomes a buried Gog-Magog
his body the landscape his nose & chin
                                        the Skelligs
a one-eyed one-legged one-armed
                                        Fomorian giant
calcified bog mummy the size of a Gaeltecht.
Later we drove to Waterville & ate
turbot in cream & parsley
crown rack of spring lamb
new potatoes & butter
with wine rescued from the undersea wreckage
of the Spanish Armada

his teeth were ogham stones
his eyes were snake stones
his veins were secret subterranean

                                        tunnels
where monks hid from each other—
spoiled monks.
                        And sea
                        & sky together there
added up to more than the
                                whole world.

GINSBERG GILGAMESH

EMBLEM:

                      ancient cottonwood tree by a stream
in a glade just outside town with a branch
outstretched over the deep pool & a rope
tied to that branch—idle youths
are eating mushrooms & swinging on the rope
diving like landlocked dolphins in
wet sunlight dappled afternoon—
when suddenly the Police arrive with a

                                       chainsaw
cut down the tree & chase the fauns away.
True story—reported by the local paper
in Boulder Colorado—angry letter to editor
from Allen Ginsberg—Spare that tree

                               —but too late.

TEN GOLDEN APPLES

Go to botanica & buy
a cauldron—red wool—barley grains—
laurel—wax—vervain & masculine
                              frankincense
circumambulate the altar three times—
gods love uneven numbers.
                    Where superstition lingers
there you get luminist scenery
                    soft & cold—
where groves are haunted who would dare
desecrate them. Ecology needs terror.
Go to the herbalists on Amsterdam Avenue
Seven African Powers—El Indio—Law
                              Stay Away
cowrie shells rum cigars chicken blood
Follow-Me Powder—*magia verde*—
                    the Dreambook of Orpheus

Didn't you
always want to become victim of magic
love slave spell as in Egypto-Greek
Magical Papyri with disgusting dead lizards
semen & blood
                    melting like wax until
you find yrself kowtowing at the shoes
of some sylvan Swamp Angel
votary of Moon & Hecate. I want
to be yr landscape—walk on me.
Yr poison is my cure.

Black magic—
                    so what—
                              nigrae violae sunt
                                        blackberries
together among willows
cool springs & soft meadows
                              lentus in umbra
down in Arcadia the
poorest rural county in the State
a kind of nimbus or localized
theosophical glow
                    trailer trash
sagging doublewides—dirt roads
vanish into Winter marshes, fade up
into lost hollows. Everything is full of Jove.
Bleak & empty. Frost & crows.
                              Long shadows.
We should've been "*both Arcadians.*" Why
are Bucolics always about desire & loss?
Horse-madness is an herb that grows
                              in Arcadia
smear it on my doorstep
                    on my bones
invoking Ialdabaoth & Jesus
all power is magic power. Carmina
means both spells & songs
                    the privet's white flower falls
blackberries are picked. And waxy plums
yes let plums be mentioned as well.
Like laurel which leaves no ash when burnt
invisible as desire itself.

The Cult of Pear Worshippers marches
toward morning's orchard with banners
& brass band. Attractive Labor is
almost orgasmic. Windfalls crushed underfoot
exude aphrodisiacs in the roofless cathedral
of Pomology—amber & ambergris of
                                    rotten fruit
Bare legs of pear pickers on precarious ladders
frotted by 18th century gentlemen in
powdered wigs & velveteen frockcoats
sticky fingers & sugary lips intoxicate
                            wasps & bees
hampers of champagne & little decorated cakes
called *mirlitons*—moldy cheese—poire cider—
socialist jizm & Voluntary Amorous Servitude.
What's good for the crops is good for America.
Orchard orgies. Tantrik arboriculture.

The Veil of Isis at Saïs is *physis*—
                            the green fuse
of Maya the month of May & mother of Hermes
salvific illusion. The Prestidigitator.
John the Conqueroo. Mandrake in
purple tights & top hat. Jesus the Mushroom.
Hamadryads & Naiads leave their signatures
on every leaf & puddle. Nature's spoor.
Aromal rays. Pheromonic lasers.
Palingenesis of rose from traces of ash.

We disguise our sylphs & undines
as Christian saints. Angelolatry is the
sexology of monothesists—its Orphic or
Uranian Phalanstery—its clock of skin.

Realizing the limestone cliffs of England
were mountains of seashells attesting to
zillions of clammy sex acts Erasmus Darwin called them
"monuments of past delight" & coined the phrase
Survival of the Happiest:
> Bios itself as
> > auto-telesis.
And *telos* derives from Indo-European root
for turning point as in axis or wheel.
O magic wheel: wind in the one I love
like fish on reel or cat that follows
> skein of wool.

They discovered Silenus asleep in a cave
grotesque in his grotto all pink on
yesterday's plonk
> tied him up with
the very garlands they'd slipped from his head
sweet *vinculi*. Stains of mulberry juice.
His songs pulsed echoing from valley to stars—
Vesper—Lucifer—beams of starlight
or long thin rays of music—flashing chains
back & forth between earth & sky.
Re-tuning the landscape.
> A saucy bit

of bondage & discipline!
> Fauns & beasts

go ludic & stiff oaks nod hoary
foreheads to the beat in Orphic rejoicing.

Iam redit Virgo redeunt Saturnia regna
the Green Messiah returns—Zarathustra's Revenge—
runic graffiti sprayed on abandoned churches

in tangle of errant poison ivy foxglove acanthus
Egyptian lilies untamed by any tractor
free the world of its long night of terror
Assyrian balm will be born of every hedge
grapes hang on thorntrees & honey drip
from dead oaks—last age of Sybilline song—
and anyway it's all late forgeries & pseudepigrapha
printed in Mexico on yellowing pulp.

HooDoo child messiah
              Amor vincit omnia
last trump for the walls of Jericho Eridu
Uruk Ur Memphis Thebes Babylon Rome
woolen threads of three colors knotted
in three places tied around the cauldron mouth
Hecate rotting goddess drifts from dead
tombs to the offering of blood
O magic wheel the Golden Age Returns.

Comix Eclogue

Given Virgilian pastoral consists largely
of lounging about in the shade any
ten-year-old on the lawn in August's
precious boredom balm would be
drawn to the Classics
                              even Classics Comics
                                        Hercules movies
secretly dreaming of repudiating monotheism
in illo tempore
                    the Classics gave us
                                permission
not to grow up. The lads were
                              planting marijuana
on the back 40—creek ran through—
cool glade near bee-haunted meadow—
et cetera. They hauled a trailer back there
no electricity no plumbing potbelly stove
candles dangling crystals—like the
grotto of Silenus in Eclogue VI.
The Jovial Omniplenum.
                              Full-spectrum perversion
sex with swans bulls showers of gold
eagles rivers trees flowers clouds
Olympian sex—incestuous paederastic
sado-masochistic fetishist lesbian bestiality—
each with its own little Mystery Cult or
annual holiday—even shit & garbage
even the complete Unknown.
                              Pastoral slides
into elegiac inevitability recalling lost
intensities in Illinois or Bumfuck Idaho

or Iowa flattened by Memory's
                    Antaean weight
its sour two-dimensional funk of regret.
Goats. Chickens. Barn cats. The
manurish perfume of proximate cows.
Dandruffy lanolin of wet sheep. Mud.
Ice. Pond scum. The bitter ejaculate
of 10,000 medicinal herbs. Rotten fruit.
Milwaukee beer. Skunk.
                    Intense sunlight
also has its own smell.
Piss on the corn. Firecrackers. Sweat.
Fecal mildew of a sagging barn.
August. Humidity. Child on the lawn
with a comicbook. A weeping humidity.

Eclogue for Hekate

Sole empress of the twilight—Woe is me
That thou and all thy spectres are outworn;
For true devotion wanes away with thee.
All thy delirious dreams are laughed to scorn,
While o'er our hills has dawned a cold saturnine morn.

If every creed has its attendant ills,
How slight were thine!—a train of airy dreams!
No holy awe the cynic's bosom thrills;
Be mine the faith diverging to extremes!

—James Hogg, "Superstition"

James Hogg the Ettrick Shepherd & John Clare the peasant lunatick
preferred weeds & squashy fens to any gentleman's formal garden. Im-
peccable class origins: —pastoral poetry by actual shepherds imitating
Elizabethan & Greco-Roman gentry inspired by songs of actual shepherds
& so on back to circa 10,000 BC.

Their hobgoblins were no mere metaphors
they were genuinely leery of glens & fens
moors of the Midlothians in the
long night before Lenin & electricity

abduction by Erlking to Elfland
idyll of the uncanny
                    rapture that ruptures
neoclassical noons
slippery schizo shadows
locked in a bedlam in Epping Forest
for 23 years or else just
celtically drunk.

The Book of
Michael Scot was so saturated with hexes
& spells they leaked out &
infected you at the mere sight of a page.
Old Vergilius the sorcerer had a recipe for
resurrecting himself as a boy but
something fucked up badly & he died.

> 'Tis evening; the black snail has got on his track,
> And gone to its nest is the wren,
> And the packman snail, too, with his home on his back,
> Clings to the bowed bents like a wen.

> —CLARE, "EVENING," FROM *ASYLUM POEMS*

Richard Dadd's fairy paintings possess this same hallucino-volkish microscopy & were also done in a madhouse. The Thomas-the-Rhymer Syndrome—the Tír-na-nÓg Syndrome—the desire to be carried away by Queen of Elfland or Erlking—desire & fear. Near where the blind harper heard (1795) on the midnight breeze music of the Tuatha dé Danaan we found a bed-&-breakfast. Looking for an elusive stone circle shown on old ordinance map we pub-stumbled through rainy Waterford woods discussing theory of supernatural music with the Hereditary Piper.

Mushrooms & menhirs
both grow in circles.
Turlough O'Carolan
last convention of Harpists
Belfast 1795.
With its metallic strings
it mimics silver moon light in
Slow Aires or silver rain
in Reels.

A Fairy Funeral Dirge from Co. Kerry

                                                however

turned out to be based on whale songs.

The Will to Power as Superstition
e.g. isn't it wiser to sell yr
soul to the Devil at the Crossroads
& cut six perfect blues 78s than
go unheralded into vague Virgilian Hades
with no one to spill blood to yr shade—
better to be victim of black magic
than none at all—to be jinxed

                                than banal—

No—

                Elfland über Alles

                                —steal away—

a changeling nation

                                into evening's borderland

with its illegal apples
city of menhirs half sunk

                                in the western sea.

What we need is a New Twilight based on the fact that—long before the
Celts—giants from Africa built with great stones & hollowed out the
earth. Like Nagas they could appear as beautiful humans or huge snakes.
A gigantesque twilight, portentous with grotesqueries

                                                        as if

seen from an artificial cave mouth
in a Renaissance garden.
HooDoo Hermeticism. Rogue Androgynous Freemasonry.
The Cro-Magnon Liberation Front.
CROM the god of heavy stones.

In the other world they replace yr bones

                       with crystal

you may lose yr gender & become

                      a hermaphrodite like Paracelsus

whose father was an incubus.

                    Or the Orsini whose ancestors

                          were bears

bastards of sea lions swans & cranes
theriomorphic heraldry—the Mermaid
& her golden comb—a superior dialectic.
Proteus the slippery gypsy hebrephrenic
morphs imperceptibly into the
world of the unseen.

                  The book falls open

on a scene of bucolic lassitudinarianism
or classic horizontality.

> *The shepherd still*
> *Enjoys his summer dreams at will*
> *Bent o'er his hook, or listless laid*
> *Beneath the pasture's willow shade.*
>
> —CLARE, *SHEPHERD'S CALENDAR*, "JULY"

To save superstition &

                  give it back

on a higher level

                  as the remedy

for terminal bourgeois consciousness
to re-enchant the landscape at the
expense of possible madness &

                      possession

there must at least be sheep.

Hence the fad for "Ghosts of Vermont"
or "Eerie Wisconsin." Cows & mud.
Nature itself has three stomachs
a Paracelsan trialectic a
distillation of quintessences.

Will dynamos die like dinosaurs
                          alchemical entropy
dissolve their cogwheels
                    luddite sabotage
restore the Golden Age of post
                          post industrial decay
infrastructure crumble
                 highways & bridges buckle
till people see smoke from the next village
but never think to visit?
                    Let REVERSION
have its way
                 gravity of the Past
magnetize all idleness & inefficiency—
forward to the Neolithic.
                          Back to moonlight
& the lonely walk home from the pub
past haunted crossroads. No cars
no electricity. Endarkenment. Hekate
of the dark crossroads patroness of
the dark side of Neo-Pastoralism.

APPENDIX A TO ECLOGUE FOR HEKATE

James Hogg Quotes

> Then since all nature joins
> > In this love without alloy,
> O, wha wad prove a traitor
> > To Nature's dearest joy?

—"When the Kye Comes Hame"

> Over the dog-star, over the wain,
> Over the cloud, and the rainbow's mane,
> Over the mountain, and over the sea,
> Haste—haste—haste to me!

—"A Witch's Chant"

The Witch o' Fife

[Another balloon song, notable for nothing save its utter madness.—Note by JH]

> HURRAY, hurray, the jade's away,
> > Like a rocket of air with her bandalet!
> I'm up in the air on my bonny gray mare
> > But I see her yet, I see her yet.

—From "Dr David Dale's Account of a Grand Aerial Voyage"
... an outrageously improbable balloon journey ... the Shepherd
sings this song as the balloon rushes upwards from the earth ...
(he) also sings a song to the Moon ... [textual note].

John Clare Quotes

And nature still can make amends.

—Manuscript Book, "The Flitting"

I love the weeds along the fen,
More sweet than garden flowers
For freedom haunts the humble glen
That blest my happiest hours.
Here prison injures health and me:
I love sweet freedom and the free.

—Asylum Poems, "Home Yearning"

Who break the peace of hapless man
But they who Truth and Nature wrong?
I'll hear no more of evil's plan,
But live with Nature and her song.

—ibid., "I'll Dream Upon the Days to Come"

For Nature is love, and finds haunts for true love,
Where nothing can hear or intrude;
It hides from the eagle and joins with the dove
In beautiful green solitude.

—ibid., "Evening"

BROOK FARM ECLOGUE

Brook Farm! Don't listen to Hawthorne
carping that philosophers shouldn't have to
shovel shit. The Pastoral is also the fecal.
Brook Farm failed as Phalanstery because
1200 people are needed to guarantee that
all Passional Attractions shall be indulged
including that for filth & squalor.
October evening in Roxbury, Mass.:
hold a seance for the ectoplasmic form of
St. Sophia Ripley. Now you read their letters
you can almost smell these farmers—
horsehair couch wet wool varnish
whale oil lamps mud tracked into the parlor
woodsmoke boiled vegetables. Haunted
by odoriferousness:—actual molecules
still trapped in old books & certain
smalltown museums when inhaled
activate atavistic reincarnationalist
flashbacks lurking in musty libraries waiting
to infest the imaginosphere with
alien spores from the 1840s
this thaumaturgic choreography
makes shameless use of childhood's
vivid agrarian mythos, e.g., lost forgotten
animated cartoons about Farmer Brown
drinking XXX jug moonshine & dancing
with chickens & cows to subversive
                              negro jazz.

Neo-Pastoralist Manifesto

I. Endarkenment

deliberate inculcation of irrational superstition & pagan animist fear of Nature. End the War on Nature with victory for fairies & black snails;

II. Secular Anabaptism

If you can't revert to the Stone Age at least you can join the Amish in 1907. No electricity or infernal combustion or telephone;

III. Escapism

Emulate the Anabaptists & drop out. Strategic retreat. Claim religious exemption from modern world. Flee to places of authentic sadness;

IIII. Impuritanism

rejects all purist theory. Strategic autonomy is made up of tactical incremental empirical freedoms not ideology. Thus we do not advocate pure revived animism but rather the re-paganization of monotheism. An impure *Santería* or HooDoo—not moral but magical;

V. Green Hermeticism

against Green Capitalism Green Party Green Tourism Green Development & other attempts to hijack the sacred color. Ecoremediation is alchemy. Paracelsan Nature Elementals. Egypto-Greco-Roman Kabbalo-Gnostic-Sufi Rosicrucian German Romantic *naturwissenschaft*;

VI. Radical Agrarian Populism

Kropotkin. Zapata. The Grange & Farmers Alliance. Ignatius Donnelly*. Against banks & monopolies. Last ditch defense of all wild & pastoral remnants. Infiltration & radicalization of tepid Green reformism to promote Green Anti-Capitalism, neo-luddite machine smashing & IWW-style sabotage;

VII. Hieroglyphic Terrorism

aesthetic sabotage. Situationist tactics (Power to the Imagination) beyond all hope of actual revolution. Totality of the Image must be attacked via Image Magic ("poetic terrorism") not in expectation of destroying it but simply to define a possible Outside—even if that Outside turns out to be failure itself;

VIII. Queer Pastoralism

"The unnatural is also natural" (Goethe)—the Pastoral Uncanny. Our relation with Nature is tragically flawed by Civilization or perhaps even self-consciousness itself. The queerness of our desire for union with Nature is symbolized by the Orphic cult of Paracelsan Tantra—sex with Nature Elementals (as attested by Cornelius Agrippa, the Comte de Gabalis, etc.) From the p.o.v. of the Technopathocracy even normal reproductive sexuality becomes perverse & archaic, & the defense of Nature a crime;

---

* Ignatius Donnelly (1831-1901), co-founder of the Farmers' Alliance and of the Populist Party; he served as a Minnesota senator and drafted the incendiary Preamble to the Populist Platform (the "Omaha Platform" of 1892); he launched the modern obsession with Atlantis with his *Atlantis: The Antediluvian World* (1882), and was one of the first Baconian/Shakespeareans.

IX. Saturn

rules both saturnine melancholia & saturnalian excess. Neo-Pastoralism embraces both. Turn of the Golden Age;

X. Thelemite Pantisocracy

Coleridge/Southey/Jos. Priestly et al. return to Nature (political Romanticism) realized in the spirit of Rabelais & A. Crowley's Thelemic Will—with influences from anarchist Arts & Crafts & German life-reform movements—Wandervogel—Sun Worshippers—nordic pagans—nudists—Nietzschean anti-authoritarians & sex liberationists. In the tradition of Swedenborgian/Fourierist American communalism & Philosophical Anarchism of Josiah Warren, S. Pearl Andrews, Lysander Spooner;

XI. Neo-Pastoralist Avantgarde

can revive the Romantic tradition of art as revolt which post-modernism is supposed to have killed—thus renewing mystic & even direct links to Surrealism (especially its late anarcho-Hermetic period) & Psychedelic leftism. Blake's "Everlasting Gospel"—the Religion of Nature;

XII. Armed Nostalgia

cultural Zapatismo. Critical Luddism. Evade the Death of Theory by oblique movements into empirical practise. Militant Beat Zen. Uprising against virtuality & mediation. Violence at an "impossible angle" to police power. We know of no actual examples—we're well into the fantasy realm here: Sword 'n' Sorcery;

XIII. Temporary Pastoral Zones

Maximize potential for emergence of Virgilian moments in everyday life. Nature will not be dead until the body disappears. The bucolic remains possible even if only as summer vacation.

Appendix to Neo-Pastoralist Manifesto

The Temporary Pastoral Zone

a version of the Temporary Autonomous Zone (TAZ) as deliberately anti-tech outdoor actual topographic set-up for ecstatic communion with Nature via aesthetic social action ranging in scope from simple picnic in countryside with songs around campfire to complex semi-permanent quasi-liberated zones. How long can you keep it going? Afternoon? Week? Season? Use Rainbow tactic of eliminating money from the TPZ. Restore Economy of the Gift if only for a day. Eliminate electricity & infernal combustion from the Zone. Luxury of dark & silence.

Leave some tobacco or spill some wine for local spirits. Cultivate the Bakhtinian Grotesque: risk some ritual. Commit some excess. Consume some phantastica. Facilitate Theophany.

"Will to Power as Art." Illusion's value for life. Acoustic instruments—the lute as Hermes's turtle. Upright piano on the lodgehouse veranda—kerosene lamps—moths batting at the screens—lemonade & flirtation.

Leave the modern world behind if only for a month at some decrepit Catskill camp. *Viva voce* readings from Virgil, Sir Walter Scott. Some desultory fishing. But define it as an act of resistance.

Psychogeographic pilgrimages & drifts to holy rustic shrines & pastoral landscapes—not as passive tourism but coherent actions for re-enchantment of the toposphere. I have in mind the woodcut in the *Hypnerotomachia Poliphili* showing the hyperpastoral "Procession of Vertumnus & Pomona" re-figured as Neo-Pastoralist outdoor theater in motion:—the TPZ as work of art.

THE NEO-PASTORALIST DIET PLAN

I.

From Indo-European root *pa meaning food in the sense of providing food by herding cattle (including pastoral unpasteurized milk). Published from our Pastorium. A Paschal Feast's Booke of Receipts or Vademecum of Gastrosophy. Al fresco pic-nics at greenswards creeksides mountain meadows: *The Neolithic Diet*.

II. (Rural Iran)

Whatever fresh herbs are in season with spring onions or ramps & fresh sheep cheese (unsalted feta)—skewers of lamb innards, heart liver kidney fat sweetbreads rolled in cumin & salt roasted over coals—eggs from neolithic chickens fried in black butter—pitchers of buttermilk—piles of stoneground wholegrain biblical flatbread from untainted 8000 year old Zagros strains of wheat—clotted cream with honey & sweet tea (admittedly the tea is anachronistic, arriving from China only late medieval period)—finally fresh fruit in season, grapes melons pomegranates cucumbers. If you're Zoroastrian Jewish Nestorian or rogue Sufi add wine (a Persian invention) with plate of olives dates dried apricots nuts pinenuts hempseeds chestnuts green walnuts almonds—bring an old Persian carpet to recline on & allow yrself an historically inaccurate water pipe to go with the sugary tea—two of the rare blessings of Civilization however wormy or unhealthy.

No Scythian picnic would be complete without the following: into a small tent squeeze all the guests then bring in charcoal brazier (grapevine charcoal is best) & heap it with bunches of Cannabis Indica—then later as Herodotus says everyone "bursts out howling with glee." Skinnydipping in any adjacent nymph haunted hole, & the actual proximity of sheep or gentle cows is highly recommended. Song panpipe lyre lute or reed flute. A postprandial nap in the shade.

III. (Maryland Crab Feast Eclogue)

Over half a century ago the hops scented
yeasty snores of uncles in hammocks
reach to the circumferences of sonic bubbles
sodden with leaf heavy humidity
mutineers of the *Tempest*
passed out on thick lawn *lentus in umbra*
might later use the vomitorium behind the barn
& come back refreshed for another bushel of
                                        crustaceans
another pitcher of mythical beer.

Steam live hardshell crabs in Old Bay & cayenne
supply hammers & nutcrackers—lots of work
for little tidbits so you keep on & on
                              eating all afternoon
with silverqueen corn picked right from the garden
cobs rolled in wasp yellow butter—
ice-packed silver keg like a family idol
watermelons stored overnight in the same ice
knuckle-thumped by judicious conoisseurs
ponderous huge dappled with fern-green stripes
sliced scarlet as heraldic devices with big
black spittable seeds (apparently now extinct)
to cool off the sanguine humours of too many crabs
red hot as alien devils. Then long shadows
begin to drop toward evening. The green
garden hose flows for ablutions—wrinkled fingers
smell of estuarial spices. Fireflies
                in the inkblots of bushes
                                are captured in belljars.

                        Night
glows with the psychotropic aura
of insectoid meat & aztec peppers
bourbon on ice & the moisture laden moon
a few bottle rockets & sparklers
the murmurous voices of distant aunts
all swirling down a vast
nocturnal funnel toward
                        sated sleep.

FLORA

FLORA attired by the ELEMENTS.

Rites of Eleusis cancelled by Xtians 395 AD, went underground & were handed down to Greek colonists in S. Italy (a.k.a. Magna Graecia), Virgilian/Sibylline bioregion with popular pagan phallus-worshipping local cults, & eventually absorbed by Androgynous Freemasonry—and then transmitted to some apple growers from Upstate New York by a Neapolitan Duke in 1861—therefore—are still being practiced today by the Patrons of Husbandry (Order of the Grange)—*lacrimae rerum*—in decaying Victorian Grange Halls by vanishing remnants of oldtime Populist farmers & their wives (Pomona Flora Demeter):—"We have the bonafide thing. Your Scottish & Memphis rites & Solomon's Temple are completely eclipsed."

The Mysteries of Flora established by Sibylline Oracle revelation 238 BC "highly indecent & obscene." Arcimboldo worshipped her as a girl made of flowers, like that lady in the *Mabinogion*. Fuseli & Blake engraved her for Erasmus Darwin's epic of vegetable love *The Botanic Garden* (1795) attended by Paracelsan Nature Elementals. Flowers

evolved into butterflies. Floraphiles
meet in private clubs where thousands of
                              dollars & ejaculations are
spent in one night on the most exotic blooms.
Dandelion wine. Candied moonflowers. Poppies.
Do you get erections in florist shops
do you wear yr raincoat to the Rose Garden
in Prospect Park with nothing underneath
fetishize the natural world in both senses of fetish
certain perfumes drive you to orgasm
Elagabalus pulls the hidden switch & buries
his dinner guests in banks of petals
nearly suffocating them. His shrill laughter.

Persephone's Quest: LSD in the kykion
with a sprig of fresh mint—an Eleusinian Julep.
                              Suddenly
Civilization simply dissolves & leaves us
garlanded with elegant weeds in a
cowpasture unchanged since the Rig Veda
somewhere in Dutchess County. A theology
of exposed genitalia. Metaphysical Pomology.
Her multiple breasts look more like pears
or testicles than nippled mammaries.

Note that Virgil's regionalist rural poet shepherds
are already sweating bad mortgages & foreclosures
wearing animal masks & their wives' calico dresses
they'll be riding out by night to tar & feather
the landlord's bailiffs burning barns & hayricks
driving tractors thru the windows of McDonalds
bombing plant genetics labs. Impossibilism.

The Good God Dagda appeared in a cloud over Co. Wicklow & told me to
re-enchant the landscape of Upstate New York—Hudson Valley Catskills,
etc.—Washington Irving country. At a local Grange Hall I met the last 23
peasants in Ulster County, including several morons & six-toed types—
an old lady bent at 45° angle who was Demeter herself—weird uncles &
aunts from the attic—hot dogs—weak coffee. It's not evil that's banal—
it's the numinous.

Hiber-Nation

Runic & hirsute we pontificate around the franklin stove like a victorian rocket ship earthbound & vestal—another crackpot perpetual motion machine—a giant iron swanboat. Pines droop like ladies in *Tale of Genji* bent low by embrace of snow. And milk. The All-Pastoral Diet. "Milky messes" as Giraldus Cambrensis described Dark Age Irish cuisine. White food. Boiled roots. White pudding. Bacon. Tea. Cornmeal mush & cream. Tinned peaches. Ice wine for ice giants. Frost patterns on windowpanes— a lost art—an art of being lost—in patterns—in glittering snow light & skull-blue sky light—all afternoon as shadows grow like trolls.

Seed catalogues: —esoteric hermeneutics reveals the Plants' Agenda: manipulating human consciousness to make the world safe for plants. On the old upright slightly out of tune one of us plays Satie's Ritual Music for Rosicrucian Mass in the sentimental style of 1911. Sleep becomes a form of political action. Ice boats like kites on skis, or sleighs with Gogolian troikas of ice-crusted percherons. Idle. Idyll. Ideology.

Cold is the principle of health & energy. We give ourselves up to narratology (XXX hard cider) & slump back into winter like an old couch. Apparent infinitude of hexagonal variations in snowflakes demonstrates that there is no repetition in theophany. Recent discovery: snow is "caused" by bizarre bacteria that ride up & down in water between earth & sky like surfers. Each flake has a living pilot.

Artificial ice was discovered by American alchemist Philalethes Starkey while investigating sal ammoniac from the Oasis of Ammon-Ra in Egypt—frost crystals formed on his glass pelican—but alas the secret was stolen by Robert Boyle of Cork, sorcerer's apprentice, who later tried unsuccessfully to sell it to the Royal Society—but in karmic payback for betraying his guru Boyle caught pneumonia while trying to fast-freeze a chicken & died (1691) and the secret stayed lost till the 1940s. Pure ice harvested from Adirondack & Catskill lakes (and Walden Pond) shipped to N. Orleans Cuba even Calcutta (in fast Boston schooners) lost half to meltage but the rest sold for its weight in silver. In highschool we heard rumors of "Cold Freaks" who only like sex in snow, with icicles, hibernudists, polar bear love. Ice palaces—temporary translucent cathedrals—were built in Montreal Chicago Moscow—1890s diamonds big as any Ritz—lit with colored torches & skyrockets—watched by top-hatted & minked Edwardians from their sleighs heaped with bearpelts. Ice Lingams. Ice-worm cocktails. Sno-cones with phosphate syrups in the old days before air conditioning in Alabama.

NEW JERSEY ECLOGUE

Early 1950s car-plus-TV suburbia crept up
like some Post Ice Age meltdown encroaching
on the shrinking continent of New Jersey farmland
like the hemlock numbness in Socrates's legs

Named for the very landmarks they'd obliterated
housing developments like the edge of night
inched toward terminal chicken farms
thru fields of dead corn & ghastly cows

Everyone was from somewhere else. Children
alone preserved a sense of place based
on secret ludic economies—songlines
leylines epiphanic meadows forbidden woods

moving at organic speeds thru
landscape already haunted by their future memories
already suffused with pastoralist nostalgia
for a mundus imaginalis co-existent with the Real

such as Summer—long as a Vedic yuga—or
an abandoned barn in June—endless twilight
boredom as freedom—enchanted boredom
of baked weeds grass stains & algic mud

Already inundated with proto-desire
they admire each others cuts & bruises
already neo-pastoralists they're storing up
animist proclivities & crypto-pagan reveries

out of remnants of a vegetal past
wading bare-legged in a swamp with leeches
smoking cornsilk behind the ruined shed
redgold as Jesus's hair in the Lindisfarne Gospels

lentus in umbra reclining on dizzily dappled
afternoon mown lawn under now-extinct chestnut or elm
doing astral projections into the brains of
long dead pirates or Scottish Jacobites

downwind from the decaying chicken farm
manure & sweet indian-grass & burning leaves
suburban bucolic New Jersey Virgils
embryonic psychonauts of 1953

Everyone was always going away.
America became a land of souls who've
lost their childhood best friends or
first loves to grown-up conspiracies of displacement

so that Pastoralism has become a Revolt of Childhood
topophilia & holy ditchweed against Progress
for an agrarian utopia that was already receding
into a past beyond any golden infancy

Feral Pastoralism—deliberate reversion
back to some ideal date like 1911 or 1795
when even light was thicker & more aromatic
like a green chaos out of Theocritus.

BLAKE/SATURN/PALMER

1. Blake

Blake's Virgil woodcuts (the only woodcuts he ever made) were created to illustrate a rather bad imitation of the First Eclogue by the early 18th century poetaster Ambrose Philips. Blake's subsequent quarrel with Dr Thornton, the dullwitted Tory school master who commissioned the woodcuts (then had some of them badly re-cut & eventually published them with an apology for their "artlessness") led Blake to kick against Virgil himself as well as Thornton. "The Greek & Roman Classics is the Antichrist," he declared—because paganism claims "the Real God is the Goddess Nature, & that God creates nothing but what can be Touch'd & Weighed & taxed & measured; all else is Heresy & Rebellion against Caesar, Virgil's Only God."

Thus in a later (1827) retrospective Blake sets his own Christian Gnosticism against Virgil's pagan pantheism—and in doing so, makes a telling critique of Virgil's materialism & imperialism. Even if we admire Virgil we can't deny the aptness of Blake's critique.

However the prints themselves (1821) suggest a different attitude altogether. Here Blake seems to interpret the text as mystical & symbolic: Nature as both immanent & transcendent, & unified by the Imagination. In other words Blake treats Virgil rather like the magical/prophetic Vergilius of medieval legend, as a "Wise Pagan" who revealed Nature as Divine Energy.

When Blake wrote his splenetic marginalia on Dr Thornton & the Eclogues he was old & sick. Moreover as a Romantic he tended to take stands against (neo)Classicism on principle. But the Virgil of the woodcuts (as opposed to the Virgil of Blake's scorn) sees the material world as the divine body (*omnia plenum Iovis*)—sees the real as the perfectly adequate symbol of the ideal, as the Imagination embodied—& thus sanctified.

For example: take the cut showing the two shepherds at their archetypal holy meal of "New Milk, and clotted cream, mild cheese and curd/ With some remaining fruit of last year's hoard" (*mitia poma | castanae molles et pressi copia lactis*: "ripe apples, mealy chestnuts & plenty of fresh cheese" in the original). This real meal both represents and actually "is" all sacred feasts—or so you would think on contemplating Blake's picture. Indeed, each of the woodcuts iconizes some aspect of Nature, like a miniature from the Duc du Berry's *Book of Hours*—but in the humble guise of a crude black & white cliché from some popular almanac or chapbook.

Moreover, Blake's illuminated bucolicism here served as the ur-inspiration for a whole school of art: the English Pastoralists, such as Linnell & Palmer—& also influenced later leftist artists like Rockwell Kent & Ben Shahn, as well as mystics like Eric Gill & Cecil Collins. In my view Blake could not simply have despised Virgil & yet still achieve all this.

In other words: the sheer genius of the art transforms Virgil into a Blakean prophet—perhaps to be imagined in the figure of the bearded shepherd "Thenot" who somewhat resembles the Jehovah of the *Book of Job* (which Blake was working on at the same time). Blake's inconsistency or paradoxicalness can best be explained by using Blake's own dialectic:—viz., that every thing has its *Emanation* & its *Spectre* within itself; or, as Amiri Baraka once explained the Dialectic, "has its good side & its bad side." Virgil therefore has both a Formal & a Spectral aspect. The latter can be represented by Dr Thornton—the former, however, as a *persona* in Blake's own "System" or Mundus Imaginalis. Thus Blake's task in the woodcuts resembles a deturnment or an "overcoming & realization" of Virgil—a struggle that resolves itself into powerful visionary art.

Swirling lines & swirling forms create a sort of Brownian movement or shimmering light in these woodcuts (& even in the preliminary pencil sketches) like that which characterizes certain entheogenic art (Huichol yarn paintings or Ayahuasca paintings), the art of the insane (Wölfli), or near-mad (late Van Gogh), or occultist visionaries (Redon, Bresdin). Sometimes called an "aura" this shimmering effect is not directly depicted by Blake but rather evoked by the "bounding line" in the double Blakean sense of *outline* and joyful dance-like *motion*. Dancing motions are typical of the woodcuts & are formalized in the cut showing a rustic family entertainment where three daughters become Three Graces, the Hermetic Emblem of recirculation or eternal reciprocal motion. See also the cut showing the shepherd "Lightfoot" approaching from a nearby hill in the pose of Hermes as quicksilver messenger service, the very embodiment of *levitas* & grace.

In *The Book of Job* this shimmering or glimmering becomes celestial, the angelic illumination of the Morning Stars singing together. But here the magic is applied to terrestrial nature—things that can be Touch'd by human senses—as well as be touched by divine fire & light: the landscape of Albion as Jerusalem, abode of peace suffused with Energy & Imagination.

These tiny vignettes appear (especially in 1821) "absolutely modern" in Rimbaud's sense—both in their gestures back toward the primitive (the crudity of old penny prints) & forward toward—say—Expressionism. They at once suggest themselves as Emblems, not in the "melancholy" sense of mere allegory but as symbols & polyvalent icons. The Blakean Emblem guides our revery before (or into) the art, so as to produce not a one-to-one code (sheep equals faithful believer) but a charged state of opening toward the numinous (sheep as energy form or even angel—but also sheep as sheep).

The up-to-dateness or eternal contemporaneity of the Virgil woodcuts makes them ideal idylls for Neo-Pastoralism's ideological revisionism. In the Pastoral of Theocritus & Virgil a doubleness is already inherent, e.g., between actual rural reality & its poeticization—between classes—between hetero- & homosexuality, etc. This doubleness functions as an unseen motivator, perhaps even as a subconsciousness, within the text. We however cannot ignore or remain unconscious of the doubleness of any *new pastoralism* in a world of "Second Nature" (or even third…) where false consciousness & pathetic fallacy are to be avoided as masks of alienation. This "Romantic Irony" is both our affliction & also simply the sea in which we swim like fish … or monsters.

To ignore this doubleness leads to the production of kitsch Blake imitations—for example Fidus, the German exponent of vegetarian Nordic anarcho-nudism—or Ralph Chubb, the visionary self-published pederast—or Khalil Gibran. Blake himself has been interpreted in this light, as a painfully sincere crackpot verging dangerously on kitsch—even by some of his admirers. Mere eccentricity however cannot be invoked to explain the sheer power of these woodcuts, their utterly convincing serious meaningfulness combined with transmutative playfulness. The cuts are not jokes but they're jocose or Jovial (*omnia plenum Jovis*)—*lusus seriosus*, "serious jokes," as the alchemists described certain of their texts & images. You can feel Blake's ludic touch in the zen-like quickness & spontaneity of the engraved lines. His irony is not a bitter limitation but a serious enlargement of consciousness.

Around the corner & just out of sight of these idylls the Satanic Mills are already in operation. The caesarism & vulgar materialism of the long 19th century (which somehow still seem to linger on…) constitute the situation in response to which Blake evokes this Romantic pastoralism. Therefore this pastoralism has a *politics*: it offers a form of resistance against Newton's Night & single vision. Blake drew a final panel for the Eclogue that was never actually cut, showing Thenot & Colinet facing forward & embracing Whitman-esquely in the meadow that seems to exemplify this *politique pastorale*—free, equal, & fraternal (or even "homosocial")—& by implication luddite. (I don't know if Blake expressed any sympathy with the actual Luddites, as Shelley & Byron did, but I can easily imagine it.) Doesn't it also seem perfectly legitimate to think of Mr B. as environmentalist *avant la lettre*, a champion of the "green & pleasant land" against the prison of school & factory?

It is precisely Blake's doubling of Virgil's doubleness that allows us such depth of interpretation. He plays a serious joke by turning Mr V's artificiality back into authenticity. The fresh primitive naiveté of the style is a sign of a successful process—negation of the negation—that restores lost innocence. (Blake of course never read Hegel—but they both read Paracelsus & Jacob Boehme.)

But the woodcuts are not one-dimensional bits of innocence, either faux or real (any more than are *The Songs of Innocence*)—rather they are packed with many layers of reflection & perception. The sign of this saturation & potency is the desire they awaken, the utopian or revolutionary hope for the restoration of the Golden Age.

See Also:

Marsha Keith Schuchard, *Why Mrs Blake Cried* (Pimlico, 2008)

Ruthven Todd, *William Blake the Artist* (Studio Vista/Dutton 1971)

The Illustrations of William Blake for Thornton's Virgil (with intro by Geoffrey Keynes, Nonesuch Press, 1937)

2. Saturn

Without wildness nearby & around it, the Pastoral begins to wither & lose its élan vital, its leylines blurred, its nymphs occluded. Blake predicted the end of the world for 1997: naked savages shooting poisoned arrows at helicopters. The long twilight of the Stone Age flickers out at last. All authentic bits of surviving sadness suddenly become simulacra of themselves—soon no doubt we'll have Sadness Tourism (in fact all tourism is a kind of mourning). Pills to evoke a trace of genuine melancholia. Neo-Pastoralism is forced to adopt a revolutionary aesthetics even if it would prefer to laze about in the shade, or pretend to be snowbound, getting high by the woodstove, telling important lies. But by now the totality of the Image itself has become a Satanic machine for production of that which must be resisted—on pain of being merely fifth-rate—or even dead.

Blake's woodcuts & certain paintings by Samuel Palmer depict, or take for granted, a neolithic landscape unchanged since Stonehenge. I saw remnants of it myself from Bro. Peter Hobson's (R.I.P.) red two-seater convertible MG on our backroad pilgrimage to Walsingam in 1976. World of Hedgerows. Thousands of years of collaboration between humans animals & Nature Spirits to produce swirling forms of energy to harmonize with the unvaryingly changing seasons.

But the pastoral world needs another world to lurk around the verges, *outside*—a wildwood climax of oaks, say, unchanged since the last Ice Age receded. Malory's unmapped green chaos. Forests to preserve the paleolithic in living amber, a refuge for bandits, witches, poachers, charcoal burners, hermits—& chivalrous fools. The pastoral world must have an exterior—the Uncanny—beyond the forest's edge.

Dubious monks also knew their share of
snow suffocating as apple blossoms.
                        The white corpse
of Novalis's beloved younger brother Erasmus
dead age 14 in his catafalque surrounded by blue roses
hundreds of blue butterflies (Nabokov's Blues) suddenly opens
eyes of solid polished turquoise—
                        the Nineteenth Century's
answer to every problem:
                        death.

3. Palmer

Samuel Palmer's entire life was transformed forever by the sight of William Blake's Virgil woodcuts. In 1825, even before he met Blake, he called them "…visions of little dells, and nooks, and corners of paradise; models of the exquisitest pitch of intense poetry. I thought of their light and shade, and looking upon them I found no word to describe it. Intense depth, solemnity, and vivid brilliancy only coldly and partially describes them. There is in all such a mystic and dreamy glimmer as penetrates and kindles the innermost soul, and gives complete and unreserved delight, unlike the gaudy daylight of this world. They are like all that wonderful artist's work the drawing aside of the fleshly curtain, and the glimpse which all the most holy, studious saints and sages have enjoyed, that rest which remaineth to the people of God." (See *Samuel Palmer: Vision and Landscape*, British Museum, 1995, p. 98.)

Palmer was eighteen, had been a painter since fourteen, a prodigy. He met & worshipped Blake as a guru, & Blake taught him how to have visions. But Palmer was not such a Gnostic as his master, and rather than seeing otherworldly beings he preferred to experience nature as divine in itself—a much more pantheist view than Mr B's.

Palmer & his fellow young Ancients of Shoreham lived as proto-Bohemian Romantics together, innocently homosocial & eccentric; they shocked the villagers & flew into ecstasies in the village lanes. Or perhaps not so innocent. "Brothers in art, brothers in love" was their credo. After Palmer's death in 1881 his son destroyed certain early notebooks of his father's which he said showed "a mental condition which in many respects is uninviting. It is a condition full of danger, and neither sufficiently masculine nor sufficiently reticent" (*ibid.* p. 20).

Palmer's "Early Shoreham" works are so extraordinary they can only be called Post-Impressionist or Proto-Expressionist or something. At the time they utterly failed to sell; probably they seemed totally incomprehensible to most of his contemporaries. They "foretell" late Van Gogh in their druggy intensity. Trees & mosses possess strange DMT-like coruscations of color & texture—everything quivering with life force. No Fuseli demons or Blake demiurges; the hills, giant moon & sun, dancing vegetation & shepherds & plowmen are themselves all holy unawares. Palmer used to call Blake a Manichean, and compared to Blake, Palmer himself appears as a pantheist monist. Blake sees angels in trees. Palmer sees trees as angels.

Unlike the leftist Blake, Palmer was a Romantic Reactionary High Tory, and as he grew older he tried to give up youthful folly (& poverty) for more conventional art (& success). He went to Italy. He got married. His Middle Period work is still excellent—& always just a *bit* strange—but far less daring & visionary. However, in old age he somehow got it back again, the trick of *seeing*. Although he now commanded a more polished style, his mature pastoral paintings & etchings are "Late" & yet soul-expanding.

Virgil was Palmer's favorite poet. Blake criticized Virgil's conservatism & paganism, but Palmer vibrated to that precise tone. For years he worked on a translation of the Eclogues (in rhymed couplets; not very good) & was planning to publish it, with ten etchings, when he died with only one in a completed version. His son worked Palmer's sketches into finished plates & published the book in 1883.

I've chosen the following late etchings to illustrate my book (the numbers refer to the British Museum catalogue cited above):

161, "The Lonely Tower"

Illustrating Milton's "Il Penseroso":

> Or let my lamp at midnight hour,
> Be seen in some high lonely tower,
> Where I may oft outwatch the Bear,
> With thrice great Hermes.

(Note the "Druidic" megaliths silhouetted by the Moon.)

162, "Opening the Field, or Early Morning"

(Palmer's only finished etching for Virgil's Eclogues, illustrating VIII 23-8.) Here is Palmer's version:

> Scarce with her rosy fingers had the dawn
> From glimmering heaven the vale of night withdrawn,
> Or folded flocks were loose to browse anew
> O'er mountain thyme or trefoil wet with dew,
> When leaning sad an olive branch beside,
> These, his last numbers, hapless Damon plied.

 # 133, "The Sleeping Shepherd—Early Morning"

Palmer described his painting on which this print is based in a letter to his life-long friend & former Shoreham "brother-in-love" George Richmond: "One of the very deepest sayings I have met with in Lord Bacon seems to me to be 'There is no excellent beauty without some strangeness in the proportion.' The [statue of the] sleeping Mercury in the B. Museum has this hard-to-be-defined but most delicious quality to perfection so have the best antique gems & bas reliefs & statues." Later in life he added,

"More than two thousand years ago the sculptor bade that marble live. It lived, but slept, and it is living still. Bend over it. Look at those delicate eyelids; that mouth a little open. He is dreaming. Dream on, marble shepherd; few will disturb your slumber." This very erotic sculpture has now been identified not as Hermes (as Palmer believed) but Endymion, the boy loved by the goddess of the Moon.

Palmer repeated the Sleeping Shepherd motif fairly often in his work, as also the Piping Shepherd—quintessentially Virgilian figures. Here by contrast with the early-rising plowman we note that shepherds have more free time than farmers. *Lentus in umbra* could be the motto of this emblem.

PASTORAL PROSE

Unjustly mocked, Archbishop Ussher (1581-1656), the Anglo-Irish theologian who calculated the date of Creation by adding up all the "begats" in the Bible, came up with Sunday, October 19, 4004 BC, at 9:30 in the morning.

We now know (or suspect) that the world is much older than this; but I've always believed that Ussher's Genesis Date must refer to *something* very very important—so important that it would have seemed at the time like the birthday of an utterly new World. Current orthodox archaeological dating systems allow us to identify that event. It was the emergence of the State—the first *coup d'etat*.

According to the *Sumerian King List* the first lugala or Priest-King was a Sumerian from Eridu named Staghorn. He worshipped the ichthyomorphic mergod Enki, whose ziggurat (the very first ever) is today a blurred ruin strewn with sacrificial fishbones.

I visualize Staghorn as a black magician or perhaps a disgruntled warrior. George Dumezil and Pierre Clastres both point out that in non-hierarchical societies the warrior gains *gloire* but dies poor, since he must share all booty with the tribe; hence he has no real political power. No doubt in the million year course of egalitarian tribal prehistory many such coups had been attempted, but all had failed to overthrow the customs & rituals of non-authoritarian Stone Age society. Since most primate bands appear to be "naturally" hierarchical, that million years of rough egalitarianism & "tribal anarchy" appear as a great mystery:—how did humanity achieve such an "unnatural" state of Statelessness? How did it prevent the early emergence of hierarchy & separation, say, amongst the Neanderthals or Cro-Magnons? If humans are by nature predatory bullies, how are we to explain this failure of hierarchy to emerge?

Pierre Clastres (in *Society Against the State* and *The Archaeology of Violence*), and E.P. Thompson (in *Customs in Common*) demonstrated that so-called primitive or archaic societies (which are never simply "simple") actually create or co-generate myths & customs that resist the emergence of the all-too-primate tendency toward bootlicking & bullying. Erasmus Darwin and Prince Kropotkin believed that the human trend toward mutuality & altruism ("love") is in fact quite natural & plays as decisive a role in evolution as any competition or violence. Erasmus D. spoke of the "Survival of the Happiest," not the fittest, and the Prince praised "Mutual Aid" even amongst beasts. Proudhon saw this mutuality as the very basis of social liberty. In any case, whether non-authoritarian sociality is seen as natural or unnatural, as genetically determined or as victory of the Imagination over misery, we can theorize the myths, customs, rituals, & taboos of sodality as constituting a million year triumph of human freedom over the thanatos-principle of fear & force & the emergence of separation & hierarchy.

So—what went wrong in 4004 BC?

I suggest: First, new techniques of irrigation had increased the community Surplus to such an extent that the Temple, where the grain, etc. was stored & shared out, became a nexus of potential power relations. Second, the discovery of coppersmithing (itself a form of forbidden "black" magic under the old regime of Stone) supplied the conspirators with superior weaponry. Third, Staghorn & other bullies allied themselves with witches & cooked up a new ideology of human sacrifice & divine kingship, with priest-king as representative of the most powerful deity or pantheon—& enslavement for everybody else.

This "revolution" met with strong resistance from the Neolithic Conservatives, as we can see quite clearly in the *Enuma Elish* or "Mesopotamian Genesis." The story of *How Innana Stole the 51 Principles of Civilization from Enki in Eridu* throws a great deal of light on the coup. See also the terrifying First Dynasty Egyptian *Narmer Palette,* which depicts the birth of Civilization as a vile bloodbath presided over by a Pharaoh the size of Godzilla.

From now on "primitive war" (centrifugal as regards wealth & power) will give way to "classical war," which is centripetal, based on plunder & enslavement of one's former friends & nearest neighbors. A new world has indeed been created, symbolized by the pyramid—a world of a few literally cannibalistic rulers & a great many fellaheen or shit-workers—& the result is Civilization As We Know It: the magic of the State.

Neo-Pastoralists agree with Fredy Perlman, John Zerzan & others who have used M. Sahlins, Bataille, M. Mauss & Clastres to argue that the Paleolithic Old Stone Age of hunting & gathering & the "Economy of the Gift" really embody the myth of Eden or a Golden Age or Hyperborea—as close as humans ever approached the ideal of social harmony, not because they were primitive & unspoiled & naturally "good," but because they resisted the bastards bullies & witches for at least 100,000 years (or a million, depending on how you define "humans") of complex systems of kinship reciprocity, potlatch, "excess & waste," "democratic shamanism," "primitive war" & so on.

Given the choice we would certainly prefer to live in a world where not only Civilization had never appeared, but where even domestication had never occurred. Ibn Khaldun put his finger on the pulse of this dialectic when he pointed out that *wild* species are always superior to their tamed or domesticated varieties—whether herbs or horses or human beings.

Neo-Pastoralists however would argue in defense of the Neolithic that the State still somehow *failed to appear* with the economic shift from hunting/gathering to herding & gardening. The New Stone Age still somehow maintained non-authoritarian social structures, like the free peasant *Mir* or village-*communitas* of Kropotkin—or the free peasant anarchists who followed Zapata, for that matter. The Neolithic polities of herding & gardening were based on love relations between humans & plants & animals—just like hunting/gathering—but with new complex & even erotic intensity. (The Nuer love songs to their cattle are enough to make you blush.) The process of domestication is at first not so much a "conquest of nature" as a new means of reciprocity & even amorous play with nature—a new intimacy.

Neo-Luddites would argue, like the old Luddites, that only a *techné* which enhances freedom & pleasure for all humans more-or-less equally, can ever allow true human individuality or "genius" to flourish, or provide what Fourier called the "utopian minimum" of luxury & gratified desire. I think that Neolithic techné meets this prime criterion.

I'm not suggesting bombing ourselves mentally or physically back to the Stone Age here … although, if it were possible, we might…; but simply trying to imagine what a genuinely non-hegemonic non-predatory human society might have accomplished *if the State had never emerged*. The Progress we've boasted about for 6000 years has proven to be counter-evolutionary in the long run, & perhaps the old pseudo-Biblical prophecy (based on *Revelations*) that "the world will end in 6000 years" may yet prove interesting, just as Ussher's Date is interesting. Myths may have euhemeristic origins but also euhemeristic fates—i.e., they may "come true."

In any case we contend that Pastoralism is not a "stage" of the pre-determined "evolution" of "mankind" toward the emergence of the State & its hegemonic separation & immiseration. Domestication does not "lead to" the State. It may not constitute the pure ideal of "Paleolithic anarchy," but by comparison with the State it still belongs to the "good old days" of Saturn's Reign. Like Fourier I distinguish sharply between horticulture & *agriculture*, which involves an economy of scale that necessitates enforced labor or even slavery. The first cultivars in all cases have been psychotropics (grain for beer, grapes for wine, cannabis, tobacco)—& the genuine pastoralist *loves* cows or sheep just as the hunter loves his prey or the gatherer her roots & mushrooms. Pastoralism is like a second Eden, compared to the economy of the State.

Not to reify the State. Gustav Landauer pointed out that the State is not a thing but an aspect of human relations & thus reproduces itself in both individual & social spheres; this in fact explains its 6000 year viral success—i.e., it does not appear ex nihilo (from God, UFOs or "economic necessity") but is always inherent in the possible failure of the social.

As Clastres said, the social constructs itself *against* a State which is always possible, given human psychic frailty & mortality. Using anthropology & archaeology as theory, we conclude that pastoralism, defined as an economy of reciprocity between herders & gardeners, lasted about 10,000 years without giving birth to the State. Then—to recapitulate—the sudden increase of Surplus allowed by nascent irrigation tech in Sumer plus the invention of metalworking for weaponry led to a coup in which the Surplus—held in the Temple—was expropriated by certain priests & warriors, with wholesale enslavement of enemies, debt peonage of peasants, & the appearance of proto-City-States in Eridu, Ur, Uruk, Lagash, etc.:—the birth of Civilization.

This war or coup against the Neolithic or Pastoral polity is clearly recounted in many texts (once one knows the key) including *Gilgamesh*, which illuminates this civilizing process—the "taming of the wild man." *The Sumerian King List* (I saw a copy of it in the New York Metropolitan Museum, in the form of a large squat clay stele giving off potent Lovecraftian vibes) tells us actual names of the first rulers, including Gilgamesh, who was a real historical king of Uruk. Money & writing provided the software so to speak that transformed the pastoral economy into the pyramidal distribution system that would eventually morph into Capitalism as we know it.

Quite elaborate architectural complexes (e.g., Göbekli Tepe, Çatal Hüyük or even Newgrange) & highly complex economic culture (weaving, pottery, domestication) therefore in themselves do not "create" the State. "Primitive agriculture" (which should be called Horticulture) & pastoralism cannot be dismissed simply as social oppression compared to hunting/gathering, as Sahlins & his epigones seem sometimes to tend to do. Horticulture & pastoralism can be seen, from this perspective, as prolongations of gathering & hunting into a creative symbiosis with Nature based on erotic energy. That is, humans developed reciprocal loves with certain plants & animals to the point of inter-species cooperation. If in the long run horticulture/pastoralism "led to" agriculture (ergo alienation) nevertheless gardening/herding cannot be *blamed* any more than hunting/

gathering can be blamed for "leading to" domestication. As Landauer stressed, there is no historical inevitability, no fated dialectic.

We now know that Progress is not by definition evolutionary—in fact may prove to be counter-evolutionary. The Enlightenment Rationalist Historical Left believed in Progress, & fell into the shit. Communism would've turned out to be an even worse ecological disaster than Capitalism, except that it failed & disappeared in 1989. However there has also existed & still exists a Romantic Left, anti-Progress, anti-Enlightenment, meta-historical, decentralist & non-authoritarian. Landauer wrote books on both Nietzsche & Meister Eckhart, suggesting that Romantic anarchism can be both existentialist & mystical. And Shelley & Byron defended the Luddites, those "rebels against the future" who believed that "all machinery hurtful to the commonalty" should be smashed. Romantic leftism is not "irrationalist" (unlike the Romantic right) but supra-rationalist. Hence Surrealism in its late anarcho-Hermetic stage lost its Enlightenment politics & embraced a non-authoritarian existentialist spirituality. Neo-Pastoralism identifies this Romantic left tradition as its own heritage. (Thus: Blake, Clare, early Coleridge & Wordsworth, etc.) Nietzsche & Fourier are valuable for their critiques of Civilization. Nietzsche of course was a great big Romantic (maybe even "the last"), & Fourier's rationalism is of course quite mad—hence its appeal to Surrealism, or to the American Transcendentalist hyper-Romantics at Brook Farm. Fourier believed that communal horticulture & cooperative federation would not merely palliate the evils of Civilization & agriculture, but would lead directly to spontaneous order & utopian Harmony—the old Hermetic/peasant-rebel dream of restoring the Golden Age, but on a higher gyre so to speak as a dialectical overcoming of Civilization. Fourier's intense communalism needs to be offset & balanced by Nietzsche's intense individualism, no doubt influenced by Max Stirner's anarchism, with the "union of self-owners" re-imagined as a "radical aristocracy" of "free spirits."

To reiterate: Neo-Pastoralism accepts hunting/gathering & the Economy of the Gift & "democratic shamanism" as the ideal polity for human society. But ideals seem redolent of purity, which we have come to distrust. Aside from the sheer "impossibility" of global reversion to H/G economy, some of us happen to value highly the Fourieristic pleasures or "*luxe*" of the Neo-neolithic—its beer & wine, its various forms of Soma—its cuisine—its Kropotkinite-Proudhonian Mutualism—its intoxicated paganism. Of course literal reversion to the Neolithic is also "impossible"—how to live without metal—without *writing*?! Paul Goodman called the bicycle the last Neolithic invention—but in fact it's made of metal. Perhaps he was simply being metaphorical? If the bicycle is Neolithic so is the foot-pedal Singer sewing machine—or the ice box. But, then, Leonardo da Vinci's bicycle was made of wood.... Actually the "last" neolithic invention was probably the hot air balloon, which could've been built as soon as weaving was invented (& in fact it may have been—in ancient China & India). What makes bicycles & balloons neolithic appears to be their deployment of "free" & renewable energy; thus—windmill or watermill but not steam mill—handloom not mechanical loom—craft not industry. What William Morris liked about the Middle Ages was actually their neolithism. Eliminate kings & nobles, & you basically get Kropotkin's Mir, the village of free peasants. Wat Tyler. John Ball. Peasants' Revolt of 1525.

Which brings us to the Anabaptists. We know that luddism is not "impossible" because the Amish today are living quite well without electricity & internal combustion. Other branches of Anabaptism practise varying degrees of tech refusal & "Biblical communism" as well. They do not "recognize" the State—no voting, no military service, etc. Their ban on tech is specifically aimed at preserving *communitas*, which makes them explicitly luddite & empirically pastoral. However, unfortunately for our theory, they are also moralistic monotheists. Is religious fervor the secret of their willingness to abjure the "advantages of Progress"? There seem to exist today no luddite communities that are "secular" or even neo-pagan. Do we non-authoritarians lack the will to achieve anything more than mere theory?

Indeed, Theory has failed us. Like Tiresias we know all but can accomplish nothing. We appear to be stuck in the text (whether print or digital), still held under the old Babylonian spell. Socialism is dead—& Society itself appears to be dissolving into a technopathocratic commodotopia of "atomized" yet homogenized consumers, linked only by the universal rhizomatic panopticon of CommTech—surveillance of all by all—each with their own car & TV & computer—Baudrillard's or Virillio's version of Nietzsche's "terminal humanity." In this situation what difference could be made by Neo-Pastoralism? Not in theory, but in practice?

Like the Anabaptists after the failure of their revolution (Munster, etc.), we suppose that if the world cannot be "saved" then at least a "saving remnant" can withdraw—enact a strategic retreat into intentional communities, unions of freespirits, to live (at least till they arrest us & drag us off to therapy) in some rough sort of pastoral or neolithicoid authenticity—not as an act of renunciation but of pleasure—not as "utopia" (which after all is no place) but with certain empirical freedoms (as the Zapatistas say) as defining characteristics. But it seems that we (who have been born so far removed from any actual pastoral life) can do this only on condition of becoming "religious fanatics."

Many severe criticisms of contemporary Green politics could be made. The environmental movement demonstrates almost no understanding of Capitalism & the sine-qua-non need to oppose it. Green philosophy grasps almost nothing of the luddite dimension of relations between technology & the social. Greenism wants to save the automobile by converting it to salad oil or sunshine. It wants to save electricity (including TV & computers) with wind & sun power. It speaks blithely of Green Tourism & Green Capitalism as if these were not oxymoronic obscenities. It offers no real solutions other than reformist attempts to interest Predatory Too-Late Kapitalismo in its feeble consciousness raising & altruistic sentimentality. It maunders on about "real food" as if organic grassfed beef at $28 per lb. were somehow revolutionary. It makes its deepest appeal to the same Enlightenment Rationalism that spawned the very mess it so deplores—i.e., it has no spiritual dimension. It is not Romantic. It is not pagan.

Here is where Neo-Pastoralism proposes a difference. We believe (again) that shamanism represents an ideal spiritual path—but we're willing to compromise on paganism, defined as a non-hegemonic congeries of sects that socialize the "shamanic" union of consciousness & Nature in terms of a polytheist or pantheist monism. In the Western tradition this paganism is best exemplified by Hermeticism, which rests on a basis of Egypto-Greco-Roman polytheism but is so syncretistic that it can absorb anything it likes, including the whole vast mess of Late Antiquity ("even unto China"), without choking. It sucks in monotheisms as if they were in fact Mysteries to be syncretized into the grand vision; that is, it proposes the *"repaganization of monotheism."*

A rectified Hermeticism would accommodate all that is truly liberatory in empirical & theoretical science by "alchemizing" it or *poeticizing* it as Novalis demanded in The *Disciples at Saïs*. We call this "Romantic Science" & we invoke Goethe, Swedenborg, Ritter, *naturphilosophie*, Erasmus Darwin, Humphry Davy & Joseph Priestly as well as the modern "complexity" scientists & quantum mystics. We want to purge Hermeticism of its gnostic dualism & body-hatred & to revivify it as "Earth Religion," like modern neo-paganism—but without excluding, say, esoteric Buddhists or wild Kabbalists or Rosicrucian Christians.

Can Green Hermeticism as a form of "radical tolerance" still inculcate the kind of fanaticism needed to inspire thousands of people to drop out into luddite communities? (Fourier demanded at least 1200 for a successful Phalanstery.) Maybe not. And yet it's interesting to note that the Amish won the right to refuse taxes, military service & "compulsory" public education by demanding "freedom of religion"—an anachronistic loophole in American law. It would be a nice irony if neo-Pastoralist anarcho-luddism managed to define itself as a Christian sect in order to "pass" as a legal entity. Some Episcopalians & Universalist-Unitarians are already experimenting with goddess worship. Why not *pagan anabaptists*?

Here we should also evoke the spirits of Leopold Kohr (*Breakdown of Nations*) & E.F. Schumacher (*Small is Beautiful*) to propose at least the outline of a practical neo-pastoral *politique* & economy for today. As I write some economists are talking about a ten-year Depression or even some sort of Kapitalist Kollapse, & it's tempting to indulge in utopian thinking, if only as sweet anodyne. Can we imagine a village or even an urban neighborhood, forced by necessity & inspired by our propaganda, taking up the old agrarian/populist causes of cooperation, decentralization, abstention from electoral politics, local production, work "bees," gardening, keeping a cow or goats, chickens & ducks, maybe even horses (if salad oil gets too expensive & cars begin to die), re-creating a social based on conviviality rather than mediation, on creativity rather than consumerism? Can we imagine the spontaneous spread of pagan cults, sects that are no longer the "opiate of the people" (as J. Wafer said in *The Taste of Blood* about Afro-American paganism) but systems of resistance? Can we picture a return of the Neolithic on a new & higher gyre of the spiral, even as the world-system of Capitalism & perhaps Civilization itself approaches some sort of End Times & final tribulation? Sure we can. Dreams are cheap.

More to the point however, can we actually propose one practical step, one opening gambit in the long march toward such a hypothetical Arcadia? Or even better: *Arcadia Now*, to paraphrase the Living Theater. Is it possible to experience here & now some taste of a pastoral future Past? Why not? The past, as Faulkner sez, isn't even past. The Neolithic actually lives on here & there in obscure & neglected corners; even bits of the Paleolithic persist. The first step toward any neo-primitivist or neo-pastoral revolution would be to conjure up the will to experience these living realities as relations ("all our relatives," as the Indians say). One summons up such will just as Cornelius Agrippa called up spirits into his ceremonial circles—i.e., by sheer magic; that is, by a sort of intoxication or self-poisoning.

And poison, too, is cheap.

HERM

the Dirty Idyll

2000 years of moralic acid
eat away at the ruined columns
     like sulphurous rain
    pitted marble
      psychic devolution.
The postmeridional faun the
garden gnome with a dildo long as
      yr elbow
yr little tritons & undines that piss in the
      olympic pool.

The first real beach in modern times was the Bay of Baiae near Naples near the Sibyl's Cave: rich Romans built summer villas—think of ochre murals in House of Mysteries at Pompei—naked ladies—boys with flutes—langorous flagellations—on the beach. Blue Grotto at Capri.

Then the Beach disappeared for 2000 years of Xtian body hatred only to be rediscovered by the Romantics on Long Island, Summer, 1981. The Duck Shop in the shape of a giant duck in the middle of a potato field. Blue swimming pool in the rose garden. Salty thickets & bleak reeds. Pow-wow at the Indian Reservation. The Raoul Dufy palette. Oysters & white wine. Half naked in the back of a pick-up truck with their dogs in mysterious Riverhead in the Pine Barrens. How moonlit sheets catch the odor of salt & iodine, estuarial, simultaneously fresh & brackish.

Holy dirt each sq. inch the Microcosm
fungal fecal fecundative primal filth
muck of swamps that flecks bare legs & feet

imaginal mulch. Smell of fermenting hay
like dandelion wine & piss. O holy garbage
Fourier consigns you to the Little Hordes
of boys & tomboys who delight in filth & messiness
rewarded with angelic titles & lavished with sweets
marching bands & parades. Poets—
scavengers at the Municipal Dump & landfill
of the archaeology of desire. Garbologists.
Scatologues. Interpreters of coproliths.
                                    O careless love.
Pythagorean aphrodisiacs. Orphic HooDoo.
                                         A crude woodcut
of Robert Johnson at the Crossroads.

Juke:
        (African word for jump & jive
        as in juke joint or box)
                        became the family name
            of degenerate Kallikak-like
hillbilly Dutch Indian Mulatto recusants
                              of Ulster Co.—
a eugenic cacotopia of petty crime
poaching moonshining pot farming incest
lived like foxes in holes in the ground
                Ramapaugh Mountain People
                Schoharie Arabs
                Vly Yonders
                Pang Yangers
                Eagles Nesters
                the Colquhouns of Red Hook
                the Jukes of Rosendale
Live Like Them. Rebels Against Progress.
Morals of Greco-Roman divinities. Bad genes.

Bad hygiene. Recalcitrantly atavistic &

six-toe'd.

Hexologists. Bucolic skulkers. Muskrat trappers.

Very early cultural influence memory—meeting a 100-year-old Black-man in Alabama who'd been born as slave (I was maybe five) in his log cabin in the hills outside Birmingham who was frying bacon on a potbelly stove by light of oil lamp. As my family is related to Joel Chandler Harris I read *Nights With Uncle Remus* in the 1883 edition. Years later I discovered that Br'er Rabbit the African Trickster was heavily influenced by the persona of Abu Nuwas in *1001 Nights*—Abbasid court poet wit winebibber pederast pal of Haroun al-Rashid rakehell libertine & magician. Thus explaining the influence of early Bugs Bunny cartoons on Surrealism. Poe & Faulkner as Gothic Pastoralists. Voodoo research of Zora H. & Chas Chestnut

Spanish moss

Greek Revival

swamp

Tom & Huck on the raft. Octaroon pastorale.
Celtic Algonkin African Anglican *Santeria*
neopagan religion for tri-racial Atlantis
with Greco-Roman Hermetic Theosophic
Moorish shrines to Nature Elementals
all around rural Ulster Co.

a new dark age

of dirty religion

syncretistic to the point of delirium
ritual pollution

rural turpitude

passional pastoral petty crime &

perversion

Captain Swing

yab-yum
        agrarian Frazierian
                fertility cults
   of the Mid-Hudson Valley.
Rife with superstition
      Dark Ages are actually
            literally dark
power lines sabotaged
      take back the night
          let stars & planets breathe
     Come the Depression
     each one ruling a Series
     of Correspondences &
        coincidences like
     phosphorescent mushrooms
      on a dead log.

PASTORAL ROADKILL

Shepherd's Funeral
                    insert reference to
                    setting off fireworks in a
cornfield in Illinois
                No Trespassing
                                    How many
petty crimes make up the Idyll—grazing
on Government land—composting w/out permit
Krishna's blue skin
                            his pet calf
                            swan
                            deer
                            dove
                            flute
                            necklaces
                            bangles
                            amulets &
                            rhinestone tiara—
                            the Hindoo
                            Neverneverland.
                            Threnody for the bees
a futurity more bitter than opium
the coming Depression as the sum of
                    all our depressions
an anti-pastoral zone for little zeks
of the gemütlich gulag
                                cooped up in
cyberkindergarten wondering
                    little lamb who made thee

BENARES ECLOGUE

Urban Pastoralism is no oxymoron in Benares. In 1970 Bro. James & I lived on a houseboat moored at a minor upstream ghat. Every dawn a fat brahmin w/ bullhorn coached a dozen would-be Arjunas with huge twirling Indian clubs & oiled torsos, waking us to another otiose holy day of lying on our undulant roof counting 12 different species of birds of prey as halfburnt corpses floated past us toward heaven or Calcutta. Up the stone stairs past tiny cell crammed with abandoned widows in white saris chanting RamRamRam to the S. Indian one-table vegetarian restaurant for breakfast—ricecakes w/ sugar & ghee—or lunch—ricecakes w/ curried veg. A few chillams with the babas at eventide—worm-eaten one-rupee paperbacks by candlelight.

Another dawn—laundresses at work "breaking stones w/ yr clothes"— ancient black dhows w/ red lateen sails arrive from the opposite desolate shore w/ cargos of sand. We used to eat at the cafe patronized by the sand-diggers, very low caste—chapattis & dhal for 50 pice. Ganja bhang & opium were legal & vended from green government shops w/ barred windows. Bhang icecream from green goodhumor men. Local Kali temple drums & bells—devil worship! Narrow alleyways lit by night w/ oil lamps of tiny hole-in-wall shops. No electricity. Shiva himself commands the faithful to take bhang in Benares. Moslems in charge of the silk trade— we hang around drinking milky masala chai getting eye-drunk on embroidered opalescent gold wedding saris with descendants of Kabir in their dim emporiums perfumed w/ extreme attar of roses.

Another day at the ghat. Every afternoon a dozen tanksized water buffalo charge mindlessly down mud slope into sacred river goaded by shiny brown boys to submerge in bliss each day new like black rubber submarines of Yama Lord of Death. Holy upanishadic white brahma bulls garlanded w/ marigolds, horns red w/ henna, block intersections & steal vegetables. Satanic goats loom up out of the dark. Vedic pastoral economy permeates/ percolates the City

fresh curds
clotted cream bedtime milk w/ thick skin
                    snowwhite sweets drowned in ghee
                                        & cardamon
iced milk w/ flower syrups—yoghurt
                    swirled w/ ice bhang & rosewater.
India equals Arcadia. Cows speak
to our spiritual DNA. Moo is
                    OM backwards.
Hinduism has preserved our very own lost
occidental polytheism. Kali = Astarte
Boy Krishna = Orpheus   Shiva = Dionysus
Zeus = Brahma   Vishnu = Apollo
                    Saraswati = the Muses
                                        etc.
all one vast pastoral culture from
                    Tocharia to
Celtic Atlantis. The Cow our Mother.
Indra rescues the cows. The waters flow.
The gods drink Soma & get all hallucinogenic.
Rig Veda describes it as goldgreen
or ruddy—strained thru a golden fleece
& mixed w/ milk—exactly like the
                    bhang lassi
at the Dairy Bar in Chandi Chowk.
                    Mornings
we take rickshaw or walk to leafy suburb where old Theosophical Society
occupies crumbling Anglo-Indian villa w/ veranda & vulture-slow ceiling
fans—browse on wormholed 1920s red Ganesh & Co. treatises on Tantra
& *Pantheistic Monism in the Sufism of Ibn 'Arabi*—free tea from kindly old librar-
ian ladies—permission to nap on the lawn in the shade of tropical trees
& English flowers.

Another night of goggle-eyed astronomy
in our cradlerocking victorian-mughal
                                    houseboat
on the river that flows from the top of
                              Shiva's head
like a gusher of moonbeams as he smokes
chillams prepared for him by Magna Mater
                                    Cybele
seated on their tigerskin in the monsoonish
                                   Himalayas
melt-off of ice lingams blue as sperm
                          Ganga = ganja
with flesh-eating sleek freshwater dolphins
sporting in its kundalini skull dark waters
snouts bristling w/ tiny teeth.

Animus/Anima/Animal

Behind beneath these eclogues lies
Okeefenokee Swamp—Coconino County.
Sunday we learned how animals practise
zerowork economics. At most they fish.
Amour fou. Talking animals 2-D as
Egyptian tomb frescoes speaking in
                              hieroglyphic bubbles.
Epistemic sweetness.
                    Proto-Oblomovs
Heckle & Jeckle—Fox & Crow—Krazy & Ignatz
sexually ambiguous crypto religious
                              epifunnies.
Phanic bestiaries. Seeds
                 of neo-pastoral ideology.

Well nowadays you can't step in the
                              same river
even once.
                 September pale ale light
goldenrod meadow in the Dutch or Deutsch
                              Wachung Mts.
petals morphing to fruit as in Fourier's parable
of Apples & Pears—wormeaten windfalls—
noble rot—color of five-basket tokay.
Adolescent desire:
                         the buzzing of drunken wasps
combined with First Year Latin.

                              "…as if
the Savior had never been born…"
in our victorian bankrupt redbrick

factory town with its abandoned canal
towpath overgrown with gingko & fern
like a Jurassic Park by Douanier

                              Rousseau

                         Spindly windmill
swayback faded ochre rickety bentwood silo
1880 white clapboard tired porch

                         for giants
confucian willows & democratic maples
plus 50 acres.

                    Black Creek Swamp
sagging rusted doublewide trailer

                         wild swans
saturnian monochrome bullrushes in
moonlit poverty of marshscape

                              dead w/ frost.
Sepia water of Black Creek Swamp
feral bucolic daguerrotype of divine

                              bestiality
olympic six toe'd incest arcadian

                              degradation
birth of the Filthy Dirty Pastoral

Animals are heraldic but

                         aesthetically poor
each toad its own escutcheon each skunk
its own coat of arms.

                         And
          what's an eclogue without wolves

what's an idyll without snakes
millipedes scorpion-gods & an

                              ithyphallic fox
Tiamat the serpent chaos goddess
& her "brood of lazy monsters"
Egypt & her jackal-headed
                    ibis-headed highly
                           intelligent
purple assed baboons &
                       mummified cats
animated by the Fleischer Bros
w/ soundtrack by Cab Calloway
Count Cagliostro on double bass
Dr Dolittle on banjo
          & Toad of Toad Hall
                    on Proustian clarinet.

Anglo-Irish Big House Eclogue

Funnel of aged yews like a near
death experience w/ light at the
end & a fair perspective of viridescent lawns

decayed stump of Norman square tower
broken open to rain   cows   moss   manure
in a stoned field of damp black thorn

Iron Age ring fort back in the bracken
where one always arrives just a
few minutes late for whatever wasn't

                      really there

myopic parterres blurred topiary
                    neglected espaliers
crazed hedges of sibylline laurel
                      shadowed
with the scent of vanished 18th century
                      children

sheep by the ha-ha—cows in
smaragdine watermeadows browsing
their eternal one-word book of
                    heraldic clover

in slow pastoral spasms in Co. Cork
near Mallow on the Blackwater near where
Spenser rotted away w/ ghostly spleen

under rock infested oaks black with
centuries of amoral sentience
cursing the rain & writing Faerie Queen

seen thru rainy windows—a landscape of
frottage & mutabilitie—soft as milk—
as if we lived inside Hollow Earth

as if we had green hair green skin &
were found in a cave naked unable to
speak any known human tongue

where it's so easy to be superstitious
to be outside drunk in the School of Night
to witness some illumination you immediately forget

something glimpsed in the unfocussed corner
of an impossible perspective as you reel
thru the park to a slow air on a

                              silver harp

a decadent eclogue heavy with unspoken desires
haunted w/ heavy colors—cupric green
                              mildew black
but gossamer w/ supernatural mycelia

delicate Ossianic emotions—like breakfasting
on bloodblackpudding & champagne—a few pints
at the rural pub that time forgot since 1911

then candlelight dinner: cream of nettle soup
saddle of mutton—claret—vintage port
by the drawingroom fire—peat—wet wool

a handful of "pookies" local magic mushrooms
a three-paper spliff of moroccan gold
& another stroll thru rain &

     alien dimensions

commemorating dead poets & otherworld musicians
famous alcoholics & the intricacies of
Gaelic vs Anglo-Irish heraldic escutcheons

then back to the house for some 1901 cognac
talk degenerates to horses livestock & adultery
outside the clouds have slyly parted

Isis-like unveiling magnificently

     maleficent stars
& whiskey whiskered moon in a
mad spin on the way home

recounting a long involved story about
a descendant of Edmund Spenser—a rabid
lady Tory who hated Travellers gypsies & hippies

won a huge blackmail libel suit in London &

     showed up
as new owner of Castle Pook (that ruined square tower
we visited earlier) claiming ancestral rights

only to discover it squatted by Travellers
& neo-pagan trailer trash in a sort of
permanent mini-Glastonbury festival

of Celtic mysteries & hashish complete
with painted gypsy caravans & horses

performing *Midsummer Night's Dream* in a

                  soft rain

an outdoor production paid for by a local
Big Farmer so his 16 year old boyfriend
could play Puck—a.k.a. the Pooka

because the Traveller children had discovered

                          a grotto
concealed beneath the castle with bones of megatheriums
aurochs sabretooth tigers & Cave Bears.

War was declared. Police. Eviction. Trespass.
The rabble retreated ceased & desisted.
Triumphant Lady Spenser moved into the

                  thatched cottage

across the boreen from her Castle.
This was where we met her—she graciously
gave us the guided tour in the rain

mentioned her intention to cut down a
thicket of blackthorn around the tower
get rid of the cows & spruce up the ruin.

Later we drove over to the Traveller's camp
& beautiful Pooka shrine in the woods
for Pan worship & wiccan druidic rites

& a few pints of Murphy's Stout & a
few pantagreulian spliffs & they told us
the Lady would regret cutting those

                  fairy thorns

and sure enough a few months later
our friend called from Dublin & told us
the gothic denouement—it seems

Lady Spenser had an alcoholic brother
who climbed one rainy night up the tower
& somehow fell & broke his neck

Now she's gone back to London & left
Castle Pook to the cows & the Pooka
& once again the druids have returned

a few details have been changed to disguise
real people but essentially this story is
first-hand reportage—an Irish Fact

from the countryside from which my great
                                      grandfather
Patrick Rion came to work upon the Baltimore-DC
interurban electric railway in 1893

my host at the time was a mushroom farmer
his house was called Castle Saffron & its
                                interior walls
were painted saffron in 18th cen. style

the old stables reeked of spores
hallucinogenic pookies sprouted everywhere
around Castle Saffron   Castle Pook

the labyrinth was overgrown & impenetrable
the rose garden gone to thorns & hips
& blue cowflies buzzed behind leaden panes.

THE JUKES ECLOGUE

In *The Jukes* (1887) we read that one of the clan used to go fishing with his underage niece; fishing being a form of "indolence," this soon led to "incest" between these "feebly inhibited" race mongrels. An obvious scientific fact.

Out for a hike in the woods behind the ruined iron mines near Greenwood Lake we come upon two "tri-racial" Ramapaugh Indians (sometimes miscalled Jackson Whites) fishing out of season—"They're making crazy love—you can snag them with bare hooks"—yanking one after another non-stop out of the creek. Or the two old Ukrainian guys fishing for carp all day from folding chairs w/ plenty of beer & sandwiches, working five or six lines & two big plastic buckets—you keep them alive changing the water for a few days to leach out the mud taste from the bottom of the muddy Wallkill— a paradisal image.

The earliest Mesolithic people of Ireland the Larnians settled beaches & estuaries—fished the surf & riverheads—collected oysters & eels—left midden heaps but no other cultural traces, so complete was their indolence & beachcomber ethos. No doubt they had some primitive form of Guiness.

I still believe Margaret Mead—natural abundance leads to polymorphous perversity—two hours of lazy fishing & the rest of the day for narratology, hallucinogenic snuff & "frequent naps."

Gone Fishing—with niece or nephew as the case might be
halcyon evenings by the weir in fading June
drooping willows suggest intimacies
as does the ritual of flaying the catfish
musty bottomfeeder fragrant flesh
then perhaps skinnydipping in
algaic amniotic tarn or electric
trembling creek.

The nymph of the
pool takes on yr niece's features, yr
nephew becomes a merboy—cold skin
& fingers smelling of fish & mud.

The Binnewaters—five small
lakes linked by swampy seepage in a vly between low hills with aban-
doned cement mines like stage sets for Wagnerian gnome choruses over-
grown with briarrose & poison ivy—cradle of the Jukes. Not one local
historical society admits their existence & the whole area is now being
developed as a huge gated community with houses starting at two mil-
lion—naturally of course all "green" & "ecological"—but in illo tempore
you could picture it as Tobacco Road with snow. The author of *The Jukes*
ventured up to this "nest of robbers & prostitutes" in horsedrawn sleigh
w/ bearskin rug. Our gothic Shawangunk Mountains are an Upstate
extension of Appalachia. Lonely misshapen cabins, caves & abandoned
canal barges. Indian remedies. County Poorhouse. Unmarked graves.

In 1912 there were still witches in Woodstock. In Pang Yang the Calhouns
still lived "like foxes in holes in the ground." Seasonal huckleberry pick-
ers. No automobiles. No electricity. No indoor plumbing. Obvious inher-
ited predisposition toward vice & petty crime sez eugenicist Davenport in
1915. Naked tow-headed kids playing in dirt with hogs & dogs. Famously
exotic looking women all notorious sluts. The pale strange eyes.

It all drove Lovecraft insane. Mixed race
Dagon worshippers—Starry Wisdom Sect
backwoods cacogenic agents of Chaos—
                              Fish People.
Ichthyolators. Crannog dwellers.
Descendents of Melusine—half fairy half watersnake.
Lumpen pastoral rural deliberate degenerates.

A cult of the Jukes
criminal bucolics shimmering with glamourie
phosphorescent as rotting fish

     in moonlight
    lilac piracy poaching
      moonshining
applejacking shiftlessness & slackology—
that fishing expedition & its taboo kisses.

We
using 1st person plural in the episcopal sense
from *pisces*—"fish"—*ex cathedra*—there are
no other believers as far as I know—
fishing rod in hand re-enact the

     Egyptian cosmogony
of divine onanism—a spilling of fish—
or some other mystical pubescent ritual
connected with trash fishing or naked fishing

      or gathering
shellfish or crawfish unchanged
since the original Sumerian Merman
fishgod of sunken Eridu circa 4000 BC.
Something Virgilian happened at yr summer camp
something Whitmanesque or Lovecraftian somehow linked
to the smell of lakeshore mud—

     neoclassical frogs
dragonflies—trance-inducing slant
    of the sun
shade-dappled shameful event with
tender trailer trash Paracelsan sylphs—
temporary Swamp Angels.

Fish is one of the Five Sacraments of Lefthand Sex Pervert Mail-Order Tantra beginning with letter "M" in Sanskrit. Now for the first time on this continent we present "The Mystic Pic-nic, or, The Five Tantrik M's according to Western Rite Hinduism":

I. Moonshine or marijuana—i.e., some forbidden form of "sufi wine" or haoma

II. Mudfish (incl. carp, catfish, eels, etc.)—lowdown bottom feeders

III. Meat. As Xtianity has no forbidden meats like holy cow or filthy pig—& neither does agnosticism—best we can do is poach some out-of-season game—or at least eat meats offensive to as many bourgeois sensibilities as possible—offal, tripe, mofongo, foetal lamb, blackpudding or haggis, possum, snake, heads of sheep or pig, "pigsfoot & a bottle of gin"—sinful meat

IV. Maize Mush, such as cornpone spoonbread Indian pudding polenta etc. The Indian version is "mudra" meaning a parched grain that is intoxicating or aphrodisiac; we substitute corn because it's so American

V. Magic (sexual), or "Messin' Around"—i.e., forbidden sex acts in which the divinity inherent in pleasure is activated & worshipped.

Note: Western Rite Hinduism seeks to re-animate classical western paganism via worship of the Nine Planetary Deities (Navagraha) of Hinduism, who are clearly identical w/ the Babylonian/ Greek/ Roman & even Egyptian planets. For example: Mercury is not only Thoth & Hermes but also the Hindu god/ planet Budh, who is being actively worshipped (unlike Hermes, one fears!) in India today. Budh is the bastard love-child of Soma the Moon & Tara the Star (prob. Alpha Pleiades) the same as Maia or Maya who is mother of Hermes & of the Buddha (who is an avatar of Budh as "Wisdom"). Tara, my own initiatic ishtadevata, is a fearsome form of Kali very popular in Bengal, & also in Her peaceful form in Tantrik Buddhism. In both religions She is the Savioress. Western Rite Hinduism seeks initiation via Hinduism to restore worship of the

Classical Planetary Deities & their "families," & then to perform *puja* or worship acc. to the Planetary Magical Rites of Marsilio Ficino as outlined in his *Book of Life* (& see also the Latin Hermetic text *Aesculapius* for vivification of idols).

                  And all for excellent symbolic & bio-chemical reasons: cacogenic agrarianism based on Land Liberty & Lazyness. Emblem from *Atalanta fugiens*—"Fishing for Coral"—

in a German mountain stream circa 1610

                            suggests

that idle angling with illegal relatives
constitutes hierogamy—the shiftless
revolutionary's *Euphrates* or Waterstone of

                        the Wise

waterlilies selfborn from lake mud
in a lost hinterland of rural squalor
loose morals & social invisibility—
Jukists—Jukites—our shame is our pride
(to paraphrase the Prophet):

                    esoteric rednecks

poling our flatboats thru shallow
lakes choked with lotus
or half asleep w/ our fishing rods held between

                        bare toes

drifting on the surface of illusions that have

                      value for life

& all just as real as they need to be.

GOAT PROSE

[NOTE: Ritual sacrifice of animals is now legal in the U.S., but I'll leave this piece as it is because the principle is still relevant: crime pays.]

Hunter's magic to effect & enact a complex relation of reciprocity with animals—morphs into the animal sacrifice of later pastoral paganism. A trace of it remains even in monotheism—halal & kosher laws. Contemporary neo-pastoralists should consider animal sacrifice. Intellectually I can think of no objection short of vegetarianism. Hunters ritually divided "gifts" of meat among their fellow tribes-people—this division continues in the pastoral sacrifice in Classical Antiquity (altho the meat is now shared mostly by priests). I've seen it done in India (at the temple of Shakti's Yoni in Assam)—hundreds of doves & goats. Gutters running with blood. Wild-ass saddhus on tiger skins. The Spanish bullfight is an obvious "survival"—the meat is distributed to the poor. The Rig Veda makes the good point that oneness with the universe means eating & being eaten— "holy cows" in Rig Vedic times were sacrificed & eaten—much to the horror of later Upanishadic reformers & Jain & Buddhist vegetarians, etc.

Neo-Pastoralism as "secular anabaptism"—as praxis not just poetics—as a life of luddite leisure & Fourierist luxury for at least a Saving Remnant of Thelemic Pantisocratists & Blakean Zapatistas. How to finance it?

It's no secret—the key is goat farming—somewhere with lax zoning. Sell the goats, alive, down in NY City for ritual sacrifice in Santería, Voudou, HooDoo, Obeah, Candomblé, Tantrik Hinduism, Ceremonial Magic, et cetera. Nota Bene: *Animal sacrifice is illegal in New York State.* And because it is illegal, it must be profitable. Q.E.D. You could specialize in lucky-color animals like all-black, all-white, star-on forehead, etc., highly prized in ritual, if you want to get into fancy breeding. Otherwise goats are fairly low-maintenance, & tough—anyway we're not talking about 1000s of goats—maybe 100—keep some for milk, meat, breeding.

It's foolish to think of luddite farming as sole support for yr household—it's too much work—it's not *pastoral* enough. Too much *Works & Days* and *Georgics*—not enough *Idylls* and *Eclogues*. This is why a little crime is necessary. If we lived in Canada or some state with medical marijuana laws … but we don't—and animal sacrifice laws are far less serious than "draconian" Rockefeller Drug Code. A little discretion should suffice. I've never even heard of sacrificial animal dealers getting busted in this business—only the customers & practitioners. One good connection in the Bronx or Brooklyn is all you need. These are yr fellow pagans, after all.

Pure-colored roosters, doves & other birds are also needed for many Afro-American & Magical purposes. I wonder if you could sell scapegoats to Kabbalists? Snakes to Chinese doctors? Black cats to Voodooists? Admittedly there are some ethically murky waters here. But—compare & contrast: a life of luddite luxury plus a little crime versus a life of honest hard work as part of the Money Machine—as wage-slave.

There are probably no more than 144,000 of us in the whole world. Fine. Let's anticipate or immanentize the eschaton or "hasten the Messiah" as the old Antinomians put it—by experiencing the luxe of pastoralism now before it's too fucking late—in our own autonomous pastoral zones. The pastoral life has always included crime (e.g., cattle raids) because in fact it's never really economically self-sufficient: it requires symbiosis with farmers. But since no real pastoral OR agrarian economy now exists in North America we must create these zones intentionally & with full knowledge of their impurity.

No true pastoralist should have to do very much more than Recline in the Shade. In the absence of a social/cultural matrix for this life—not to mention its economic implausibility—some small crime must take up the slack. Plus, as Nietzsche says, it engages the will to power & energizes life in general to overcome a few "stupid little laws." Thanks to the radical heritage of the Whiskey Rebellion the model American pastoral crime would be moonshining (originally of course an alchemical discovery)—but there's no market for it here. Sacrificial goats however are greatly in demand.

Pastoral Pigeons

Persian dove towers—3 or 4 storeys high cylindrical & open in the middle (like a thick walled chimney) pierced w/ thousands of cotes in serried ranks around avian adobe phalanstery or babel, delicate white wedding cake frosted w/ guano, with a gate to dig out the lode of nitrates. The *Book of the Ring of the Dove* symbolizes the circumcised Moslem penis & the nest of Aphrodite. Squab pie. When the passenger pigeon went extinct America was suddenly no longer pastoral. Messenger pigeons are luddite CommTech. Fourier praised the pigeon post—it was later perfected during the Paris Commune when Hermetic hot air balloons escaped the siege carrying pigeons, which could then fly back into the City with messages tied to their legs in little capsules. Pigeon coops on Lower East Side tenement rooves—*rus in urbe*—every evening emit their acrobatic pearly flocks to catch the last sun on aeronautic breasts.

EQUITES

Scythians w/out their horses are like centaurs
cured by cut-rate psychotherapists—half human
                                        half nothing.
Twelve thousand years of co-evolution down the drain.
There is no chivalry without the horse—no
                                        psychic north.
Organic speed vs. machinic speed—the difference
is life itself. Karakorum the capital city of the Khans
consisted entirely of yurts house wagons & horses
when you went back again it had moved
                                        vanished
over the horizon's edge. Gone to Croatoan
to become White Indians. To liberate Bermuda
                                        for the monsters.
Born of the dying Medusa, Pegasus freed the
Hippocrene waters on Mt Helicon &
                                        stoned the masses
—winged horse of the Scythians howling with glee
white horse of Ali or Caligula or Robert E. Lee.

AGITPROP

as the text itself is a false Arcadia
spleen
      neurasthenia
            the Mithraic basement
megalithic crawl space
          under hollow hill
      IDLE REVERY rather
      than IDYLLIC REVELRY
              Gate of Ivory not
              of Horn etc.

            larvae or *qlippoth*
as the Kabbalists call them—invisible
          pornographic
             glowworms
phosphorescent maggots
        SciFi succubae
in the shapes of shepherds & dairymaids
            mushroom flashbacks
collaboration with Kulaks
      infantile deviation
        false consciousness
& other discredited rubrics of a century
so past it seems downright mauve
      & tarnished silver

    Most days a
        yawning abyss
of ennui & decrepitude
      slowly dissolves
        in Dragon Well Tea

                    clouds in Sung landscape
                                or Persian miniatures
in lavender ink on blue cartes postales
White Peony Tea
                    tarnished pewter clouds
                        rotten ice &
                        isolation
hindoo hoodoo candles & grisgris
from the grave of Dr Brink of Kingston
against witches bankers lawyers
                    telepathic rays beamed from satellites
(the glass panopticon)
                                against being understood
                                        to be opaque
as Basil Valentine—silurian
                    as Philalethes Vaughan—gnomic
                                as the Mao Shan Tractates
to decode dakini tadpole scripts
in the style of Mallarmé
                            (or at least his typography)
so the calligraphy comes out white on
                                black pages
slow & dirty as tombstone rubbings

a bat cave of mere stuporous carouse
an impotent pissing in the snow—a
            whistling past the graveyard of
                        Zarathustra's Revenge

So why should you still feel like José Martí
teaching Spanish at a girls school in rural
Upstate NY as if somewhere an island
were waiting to take to the mountains

                              in honor
of a single pastoral song

                    because behind
                         beneath
                         or prior to
the utopian text & its unsavory aura
of artificiality & inauthenticity lurk
                    remnants of
resentful hermitages & the alchemy
                         of unhappiness

Pan slogging up to his waist thru thick earth
toward a pavilion where a young faun
w/ erection spies on a sleeping nymph
from whose mossy breasts the fountain spurts
                              splashes
—secrets of Capri Caprarola those capricorny
capricious goatish priapic topospheres of
the bucolic grotesque
                    et in Arcadia ego
                    our Complaynt
will warp young minds like a Dowland
                              arpeggio
immanentize the eschaton like a Tijuana bible
stretch out one golden afternoon like
                    E.C. Comics
into a temporary eternity

VIOLENCE PROSE

The word pastoral almost always seems to mean peaceful, as in a "pastoral scene," but in Alba (ancient Scotland) & Albania & other wild remote rugged backwards sheepherding mountain or border cultures, pastoral violence occurs in a context of tribal anarchy— a system usually regulated only by some ancient unwritten *code duello* or *lex talionis*. Eventually everyone's living in isolated stone towers guarding their herds with flintlocks & sabres. Hatfields & McCoys—the clan feud—*razzias*—livestock rustling—the *táin* or cattle raid—assassination--& the occasional small pitched battle or siege ... sometimes one takes to the hills ... barns are burned, etc.

Tribal anarchy in its pure form exists where no central State power has yet appeared, where the Code is the only law & the result is the endless fissipation of power through "democratization of violence." In time this situation becomes the tribal definition of freedom itself. When the State finally appears & tries to subdue the pastoralists, they immediately turn outlaw rebels, social bandits, land pirates, Jacobites, nightriders or secessionists.

In 1969 (when I passed through) the Khyber Pass was actually controlled by uncontrollable Pathan tribes who allowed the border to function in exchange for tribute. All the men were armed with bandoliers & replicas of WWI Lee-Enfields lovingly forged (in both senses of the word) by local craftsmen who shared the bazaar with little mudbrick cornucopias of smuggled & stolen luxury goods beneath treeless black split crags, carrion eagles hovering in hot metallic blue sky: hashish, fake Lugers, Japanese radios, opium, flintlock rifles, Chinese tea kettles, daggers, binoculars, ammunition, plastic clocks, plastic sandals, indigestible mutton, greasy rice & bowls of cardamon-scented syrupy green tea.

The Kurdish Qadiri dervishes I met in Sanandaj (1972) were eating glass & scorpions, handling snakes, piercing their cheeks with skewers, dashing their heads against the wall, plugging themselves into live sockets—all totally unscathed & magically unscarred. This is the spirituality of free mountain warriors, & no doubt represents the persistence of archaic & shamanic material. (Elsewhere in Kurdestan you even find Ahl-i Shaytanis & Yezidis—actual Devil-worshippers.) So it still goes in remote mountain valleys with real pastoral economies.

In the Border Marches between England & Scotland in late medieval times banditry, cattle-raiding, heresy & feuding came to define an entire culture—a way of life later transported to the US southern Appalachians—based on the idea that "whiskey & freedom gang tegither" as Robert Burns said—the jug of moonshine & the flintlock. My own ancestors the Cranstons flaunted on their coat-of-arms the heraldic motto "Thou Shalt Want Ere I Want"—the slogan of aristocratic burglars. A certain poetics always accompanies this kind of life, typified by the "Border Minstrelsy" collected by Scott & Hogg—dire ballads of revenge, murder, mayhem & fairy abduction. (Typically, the Cranstons were afflicted by a hereditary "goblin butler"; see Scott's *Lay of the Last Minstrel*.) Violence plus poetry equals militant pastoralism.

Tribal anarchy never expands beyond primitive warfare; it never accumulates power. All members of Highland clans consider themselves noble, down to the last goatherd—*armigerous*. Kurds, Pathans, Baluchis, Montenegrins, Albanian & Scots-Irish hillbillies—all are noble. All are free. An alliance of such tribes can launch a nomadic war machine by enslaving whole sedentary populations; the tribesmen then become true aristocrats. Celts, Goths, Visigoths, Franks, Normans—all undergo the transition from bandit to feudal lord. But then, as Ibn Khaldun remarks, they grow decadent, urbanized, educated, sophisticated, effeminate—like the Vandals in Tunisia & their effete Court Poet, Dracontius, with his opalescent epicules—all swept away by the Byzantine Navy, leaving behind them only the occasional blond greeneyed Berber shepherd.

In its ahistorical manifestation as ordered chaos, pastoral feuding can be seen as a social means of preventing any emergence of the State with its alienation & separation—therefore as prolongation of hunter/gatherer primitive war into the pastoral/ horticultural economy—centrifugal in relation to accumulated wealth & authority—the chief's power limited by the Code's potlatch rituals of extreme generosity (cf. Beowulf & his feasts & ring-gifts) & the democratization of chivalry—he must give away his own war booty in huge blow-outs of meat & mead; no clan member must go hungry; talented warriors & bards are his companions, not his servants; each hot slice or joint of wild or pastoral beast must be handed to the proper hero or poet in the proper order—or else duels of honor will have to be fought (honor here meaning the autonomous self whose freedom is the sole object of the whole system).

Pastoral violence literally redistributes the Surplus so no clan gains economic power over another. Typically cows, horses & women are stolen & re-stolen in an extreme version of Lévi-Straussian exchange:—a socialism of rustlers in which eventually a tragic existentialist sensibility will express itself in art—in Scythian gold—or the Scottish lay:

> 'Twill charm the mermaid from the deep,
> Make mountain oaks to bend and weep,
> Thrill every heart with horrors dire
> And shape the breeze to forms of fire."
>
> (JAMES HOGG, THE QUEEN'S WAKE)

A Gothick Orpheus.

Genealogy is a pastoral artform usually expressed in woven patterns such as tartan plaids or other so-called abstractions as Carl Schuster proved. The earliest plaids are found wrapped around dry-frozen salted mummies in Central Asia, e.g. Tocharistan (W. China), where redhaired blue-eye'd barbarians circa 1000 BC spoke a language closer to Celtic than to Persian or Sanskrit. The plaids were loomed in "Scottish" weaves. (See *The Mummies of Ürümchi* by Victor Mair et al.) Ergo one must reject the revisionist debunkers who claim that Scots tartans constitute an 18th or even 19th century

Romantic fakelore pseudo-tradition. Similarly, I believe "late decadent" Scots heraldry actually preserves archaic totemic memes. For instance, the Cranston escutcheon (a "punning crest" showing a *Crane* In Its Vigilance with a *stone* in one claw) refers to Celtic crane shamanism, eerily similar to Chinese Taoist crane symbolism: magicians ride on cranes or become were-cranes, keep sorcery kits in crane bags, etc. Compare with the Egyptian ibis, theromorphic avatar of Thoth-Hermes.

Ireland's hundreds of tiny kingdoms were erased & Celtic aristocracy replaced by Normans & Brits, but the pastoral economy never changed from pre-Celtic days till the Famine of 1848. And so the spirit of agrarian violence never died but was re-appropriated from the oppressors in drunken riots w/ shilalleghs at remote shrines of forgotten saints & magic wells ... or by nightriders in white robes—arson & ambush—the familiar tactics—terrorize the landlord's agents—& of course, compose long sad ballads & stirring epics.

In Virgilian S. Italy & Theocritan Sicily the Pastoral Code degenerates into Mafia shadow-government of the people against the State—with the usual feuds & feudalism transposed from rural clans to "crime families," & money replacing cows as unit of value. But periodically an earlier & repressed energy re-emerges amongst shepherds & peasants, hopeless bloody uprisings against State power followed by decades of social banditry—and naturally, songs. Sicilian mafiosi & Mexican narcotrafficantes pay to have heroic ballads written about themselves, recorded & played on local radio stations. Parry & Lord recorded illiterate bards in 1940s Yugoslavia still working in true Homeric vein. Pastoral poetry—primitive slams or bucolic amoebions—are still going on in the shitkickin' outback of Yemen, land of sheep & tribal anarchists, nest of heretics in walled mud citadels, living off the incense trade since 2500 BC. (The Somali pirates might be listed here: pastoralists who've taken to sea. According to a Somali friend of a friend of mine, "We Somalis don't like governments & we don't want one!") Tribal anarchy may not be proper anarchism—but it's certainly not the State.

Jefferson's tree of liberty that needs a periodic watering with blood is a concept so pastoral—so Appalachian—so Scotch-Irish—that one wonders: how could a tidewater Virginia gentleman have imagined it? Answer: maybe Jefferson was schizo. Maybe it was some kind of secret Freemasonic teaching. Who knows? But one of his multiple personae was our first (& maybe only) pastoral president, envisioning a nation of free agrarian yeomen—ambiguous godfather of radical populism & American Individualist Anarchism (the "unterrified Jeffersonians" as Benj. Tucker called them). As someone involved in Shays Rebellion put it, Western Massachusetts "reverted to the state of Nature." So did the Green Mountain Boys of the independent Republic of Vermont; so did anti-Federalist radicals who condemned the Constitution as counter revolutionary—as did the Whiskey Rebels of 1794; so did Tom Paine & the Masonic Druids of New York, freethinking deist radical democrats, American Jacobins, Bavarian Illuminati—allied with bankrupt farmers, moonshiners & victims of fraudulent land speculation schemes launched by Bob ("The Banker") Morris, Alex Hamilton, & the nascent Wall St. Money Interests (Gen. Washington was heavily invested).... Basically the whole American Revolution was one big real estate scam. Its leaders were rich conservatives for the most part, even monarchists, except for a sprinkling of leftwingers like Sam Adams, Mr & Mrs Warren, or Richard Henry Lee, 10th President of the US Continental Congress under the Articles of Confederation. These folks were the reds in the red white & blue.

[Digression: some quotes from Lee:]

> "The spirit of commerce through out the world is a spirit of avarice."

> "The first maxim of a man who loves liberty should be, never to grant to Rulers an atom of power that is not most clearly & indispensably necessary for the safety & well being of Society."

Lee opposed the Constitution because the

> "greatness of the powers given, & the multitude of places
> to be created ... will produce a coalition of monarchy men,
> military men, aristocrats & drones, whose noise, impudence &
> zeal exceeds all belief."

[Material here for a Poundian but anti-fascist Presidential Canto!]

Above all we New York neo-pastoralists like to evoke our Calico Indians, nightriders in the Anti-Rent War of 1845, praised in a footnote to the Communist Manifesto, joined by Irish & English Chartists in exile—terrorists we'd call them now—tarring & feathering landlords' agents. To them, "Down Rent" meant *abolish all rents*. Burning barns & blowing tin horns to summon the tribes—meeting in isolated taverns or glades in the forest—conspiring to save Moses Earle's farm from foreclosure. A hundred masked riders in drag—shots are fired in a meadow outside Andes—sheriff Osman Steele falls from his horse—the arrogant bully who'd boasted earlier that day in Hunter's Tavern that "Lead can't penetrate steel."

Coincidentally all this occurred at the crest of American Romanticism smack dab in the middle of the Hudson River School of Art & the mythic urgrund of Irving & Cooper—(not that *they* appreciated it). Now all that remains is a WPA mural in the Delhi post office & the occasional costumed re-enactment pageant. I've been to Hunter's Tavern & Earles's farm, seen the shabby cabins of Calico Indian chieftains rotting away in Columbia Co.—the poor churches of Down-Renters in Rensselaer Co.—& made pilgrimages to view one bent tin horn or calico dress in a public library, or a fake mask from the 1895 Commemoration, & even the rock in the forest where torchlight convocations & serpent dances were held & the Down-Rent flag was stuck into that very hole in the stone, a vanished Excalibur. I've been to Steele's ostentatious Egyptian obelisk in Delhi Cemetary, & Chief Big Thunder a.k.a. Dr Smith Boughton's cracked headstone in

Hoags Corners—he was jailed for insurrection after the rally in Smoky Hollow, "shouting shooting weaving about with cow horns thrusting from fierce painted masks & animal tails bobbing on their backs" singing Down-Rent songs: "Take up the ball of revolution where our fathers stopped it"; and, to the tune of Old Dan Tucker:

"We'll tar your coat & feather your hide, Sir!"

And now nothing remains but a few rusty historical roadside markers, locally printed pamphlets by amateur historians—not even a living memory of the last agrarian uprising in New York State—our very own *Tierra y Libertad*—our "Chivalry of the Nineteenth Century," to quote the title of a contemporary account.

And now Steele has triumphed at last: a technopathocratic corporate police state of repressive tolerance & consumer ecstasy renders popular violence meaningless, recuperates it as Spectacle or simulates it as pure television. Even blowing up cellphone towers disguised as trees, or cancerous power lines that scar whole forests, burning down GM crop labs or torching SUVs, however emotionally gratifying, appears pointless as any absurd existentialist *acte gratuit*—yet another manifestation of neo-pastoralist impossibilism—another antiquarian daydream, remote as the *Morte dArthur*.

SPORES

1.

"Freedom & whiskey gang tegither" (Robt. Burns)—as do
moksha & *majoun*.

2.

   Terrorist Project:
release Canadian wolves in the Catskills
       & Adirondacks
send no communiqués to media—let our
relatives the wolves speak for themselves
      like the
trumpeters of Manitou
     because sheep w/out wolves
& dogs to protect them are just
karmic non-entities.

3.

Smell is the 5th axial quintessential sense, aetheric & subtle,
between earth-touch & water-taste on one hand, air-hearing &
fire-sight on the other.

4.

    Novalis wrote Pollen
I write Spores—infectious yeasts
that will turn yr verbal dough into
swollen loaves hidden in baskets
     under napkins
only revealed to initiates
    —fungal phalloi
     —baroque pearls.

5.

        protoplasmic rhumba
bulging with gardenias
               choked
with ermine rhinestones like the
dragqueen of the Mysteries
                   Persephone
gathers wildflowers w/ the Sea Nymphs
briar-roses saffron-crocuses violets irises
hyacinths hundred-blossom'd narcissus
each minicosmos of animacules
atomies & quantum indeterminacy
a cauldron of
            pursed masochist lips
hungry for bee-stings.

6.

At least the eclogue could advocate violent overthrow of the
State & thereby elevate itself from empty blather to actual crime.
Death to anti-pastoralism, then.

7.

Vagueness hides power
as clouds conceal accumulations of vajra—
dead moths reveal no potent morphologies—
Theory itself is badly haunted.

8.

Some titles:
The Wreck of the Eclogue
"The Viol, the Violet & the Vine" (E.A. Poe)
The Ideologically Rigid Neo-Pastoralist

Hillbilly Zen
Tao of the Jukes & Kallikaks

9.

The County Fair always promises
some revelation Circus of Dr Lao
tunnel of love with real love
romance with 4-H Club
blue ribbon winner—
                              platonic apple pie
ideal chicken stew w/ dumplings
by Ladies of the Grange or
Methodist Church
                              some spectacle
of absolute animal pulchritude
or rural virtue
                    or giddy
forbidden fun unknown since
guilty childhood. But
it never delivers.

10.

Somewhere Thoreau predicts weeds & fungi breaking thru asphalt
dissolving parking lots, kudzu engulfing gas stations, & "at last the Red
Man returns…." Such fantasies can only be brought on by nausea &
suppressed panic.

11.

We need de-education camps
to de-brainwash us back to our childhood gaze
—not only poor but cheap—ideally free—
                                        or stolen.

A luxury of absences. Li Po pawns his overcoat

                          for wine.

Snow falls into black pool. Crows cross
blank field in mud season

                in a tearful

light.

12.

            America—A Prophecy.
Your cause is hopeless—second childhood
youthful folly dishonors its already
unsavory reputation. The curse of

                    neoplatonism.
An aether dream. An anesthetic revelation.

13.

            Turn over a clod
            Disturb a god
unlike Baudelaire who never got any farther than Belgium
a dazzled Rastafarian
been to the bog & smelt the psychotropic turf
mildewed thatch—moss in the kitchen sink
            Stoned drunk or
            bhanged up enough to
take longshot pascalian odds on the
real existence of matter as sentient energy
because if you say the Pooka was only
mist & moonlight I'd reply sure what else
would the Pooka use for a body
               Could the banshee be
               enfleshed in poetry?

14.

        Follow banish'd Night's

withdrawal in shame

        veiling herself in

            starry burka

toward the last povertystricken pockets of

dying darkness

        down into

           sewers flowing beneath

palaces & jails of the Abrahamic Police

6000-year-old stone soup

of damned but unrepentantly

        poetic facts.

15.

IDYLL: —a nexus between consciousness & nature experienced by more
than one person—shared and simultaneously & deliberately poeticized,
as Novalis would say. A poem that we live in.

16.

For example in honor of Paul Goodman
& Guy Davenport, late lamented
pastoralists *par excellence*, we accept
not only the bicycle but also the cooler of

        bottled beer

the lawn chairs

        etc.

17.

Without the poison of Eros the Pastoral Autonomous Zone can't be considered really pukka. Luckily this erotic dimension can be provided by nature's presence under the aegis of Nature Elementals & demi-deities—symbolic co-amorousness of nature & human awareness. A variant of the Temporary Pastoral Zone would be the hunting trip— "venery," meaning both the art of the hunt & the art of Venus. Language languaging. Hunting is NOT a precursor to war as so many neo-con anthrop's believe, but rather another kind of violence altogether.

18.

When the Church gained total power it became necessary to hide the role of entheogenic ceremonialism as the path of attainment in pagan mysteries—altho we hear rumors of it amongst the "witches" & satanists as pagan remnants (v. M. Murray & C. Ginzburg). Now the Knowledge is once again available but the sacraments themselves are declared illegal. Their very illegality is a sign of their spiritual efficacy. Consciously directed (e.g. at Eleusis) the Soma Sacrifice is the *upaya* or "skillful means" of attaining the pastoral experience of immanent divine Nature.

19.

Topophobia

a rain of heavy water

$$[H_3O]$$

on deserted esplanades by di Chirico
neo-classically sterile as

a travel nightmare

with miles to go.

20.

       red dust as

       Han Shan calls it

the all-too-human—the death of Pan

in the dromosphere of a global

               accident

            zone.

21.

We look at nature now with the heartbroken clarity of a convicted
prisoner being driven off to jail & staring out the black maria's back
window at sky & clouds.

22.

Our neo-pastoralism is tainted with the

                   valedictory

elegiac threnodic hymnody of obsessive

attempts to make language itself

            take the place

of place. Zion in a strange land.

Literary Rastafarianism.

Organs without a body.

From this perspective a picnic

            in the woods

becomes a revolutionary act.

23.

Send some Elementals

to elementary school to take over

impressionable brains like daemonic possession

by insalubrious comic books

                              —a
generation of lycanthropes
weaned on green revanchism & resentment
from Hollow Earth—changelings.
Comicbooks about Hiawatha Johnny Appleseed &
                              the Unabomber
sneaking out of their houses at night to meet
                                        in the woods
for unspeakable cults of bakuninism &
                    militant deschooling.
                    Children of the Corn
                    Zéro de Conduite
Village of the Damned types with ESP &
rudimentary shapeshifting powers.

It was this book SPORES that called you
conjured you & fore-ran you
                    O collective messiah—
John-the-Baptized you & sent you
these fairy tales with their strange
                    woodcuts
that first awakened your latent hatred
                    of the modern world.

MUD SEASON

Nine InstaSonnets

I.

Mud Season weasels into Winter's R.E.M.
like a cold wet hand in its pyjamas
like cold phlegm in the morning when
you wake in draculesque flaccidity
with an amoeba for your coat-of-arms
& Dr Leary's brain on the rocks.
Sheep dipped in tar against the worm
cacachrome still life of merds & words
used shrouds of yellowing snow shards
& gangreen'd ice. Yr subscription has expired.
When suddenly with a sip from the jug marked
XXX you seismograph an impending thaw
a loosening of underground bowels & reins—
H.P. Lovecraft's face replaced by a giant orchid.

II.

Every morning you wake as a decayed monotheist
combination Hawthorne & Stephen Hawking
hacking up ideological catarrh like a
Hindoo Hotel at dawn—yogic mucus.
Arcimboldo could paint you as an allegory
of Mud Season—melting icicle for nose
dead sleeping willows for falling hair
fungal stumps of teeth—three more days of this &
you'd be the wicked witch of the west's un-
resurrected avatar—creature from the

                              brown lagoon—
when suddenly the Green Fairy touches you
with her wormwood wand & you become
John Toland (1670-1722) Masonic Druid of Belfast
Knight of Jubilation & coiner of the word

                              Pantheism.

III.

Marx must've visited some Polish shtetl
in Mud Season when he remarked on "rural stupidity"
since he'd never been to the Catskills—
nevertheless magically linked via footnote eleven to
Communist Manifesto where Engels mentions
NY Anti-Rent War of 1845 in warm
but guarded terms. They thought
a lot about Upstate NY while reading
& annotating Morgan's work on the Iroquois
but they were never here in Mud Season
except maybe ectoplasmically. Snow
has its own intelligence but mud's moronic
or anarchic—subversive of form itself
dialectical nightmare quagmire pig swill of ideas.

IV.

Naked sylph coated in mud—not
fecal clots but thin as second skin
living slime—the physics of which
is a quantum mechanic's paranoid or
perverse illumination—neither this nor that
like the scat of Schrödinger's Cat—
all musky as rain on rotten ice &
murky as morning miasma—harbinger

                          of snowdrops

& bluebells to come—Mud Season divinized—
Angel of late February thaws & the
breakdown of moral standards—

                       sexual mud

to lick like Sacher-Masoch from toes & shins
like a melted sachertorte of Viennese

                         subconsciousness

awash in the residue of Aztec dreams.

V.

Dregs of turkish coffee in upended cup
form nilotic deltas & ferny emergent Mandelbrot fractals
peninsulas & isthmuses of black oneiric frost patterns
on the window panes of possible becoming—

                              divination by mud.

In Persian & Erse springs are called eyes
of the underworld—every puddle another
drowned City of Ys haunted by microscopic
mermaids frog sperm delicate
interstices of earth & tinted ice

                              —suddenly

clusterbombed by childrens' rubber wellingtons
little Jackson Pollocks making splatter patterns
of an absolute Present as slices of eternity.
Here's mud in yr eye O Cyclops of Winter
with yr bad gypsy cards & 2-D versions of futurity.

VI.

Neither winter nor spring—barzakh as

Ibn 'Arabi calls it

in-between-season or liminal realm of the
Blakean Imagination—from unconscious muck
to Lunar Mansions—from swine to pearls
from mulch to Taj Mahal.

Woodsqueer

with cabin fever we had to cut ourselves
free of our longjohns with garden shears
like lascivious Lapps who can always
whistle up a wind.

River ice

cracks like a tortoise shell in the Shang
Emperor's hand—far away on the frontier
the frozen dessicate saline Gobi dissolves
revealing the mummy of a Caucasoid shaman
buried with his cannabis indica pouch

for 2700 years.

VII.

To Dream of Mud signifies imminent
immersion in the Dalíesque timescape
of Freud's own badly suppressed fears of
"the tide of black mud"—ghosts—alchemy—

all that

Nordic *schwärmerei* that threatened
to seep into the basement of psychiatry
& underwhelm the necessary discontentments
of Biedermeier Civilization—opaque mud—
black mud being slang for opium—the opposite
of cocaine's pure Enlightenment rationalism
opium's limpness vs. coke's virility:
Freud's Frankist & Sabbatai-Sevian ancestors
emerging like Dr Franklinstein's protégés from
behind the African masks on the mantelpiece.

(Lucky numbers
13, 23, 93)

VIII.

Mud Season is itself nostalgia season
locked bundled in our Dutch bed cupboards
with footwarmers & novels by John Cowper Powys or Proust
or Jean Genet—poets of muddiness & squalor
writers you can imagine actually fucking the mud itself
Erskine Caldwell—Li'l Abner & his pigs
corncobs in the privy—where the sweetest
honeysuckle grows—delicious degradation
sexual thrills of class treason

                    whitetrash *weltanschuang*
rural lumpen recalcitrance &

                    permanent unemployment
—psychedelic mud. Intoxicating dégringolade.
A themepark with mud rides & mud baths:
MudWorld—the zen of letting it

                    all

                        slide.

IX.

Estuarial Pastorale—brackish backwater
Jersey Pine Barren sawgrass & silt
crawfish & bayous—voudoun country.
Mesolithic shellfish scavenger midden heaps
& beach plums. Waterlands. Fens.
The Marsh Arabs of Iraq—an entire culture
based on reeds & mud. The stench
of Innsmouth sandflats when tide's out
like bodily secretions. One man's eldritch horror
is another's banquet of pheromones—

                         a poetique of boue

an imaginaire of mud—salty as blood
but soft as boudin w/ fried apples
or squid in suo tinto w/ moro rice
or lobster molé w/ Guinness & champagne.

CORN ECLOGUE

disguised as one of those 1940s Sister acts
close harmony slinky cocktail gowns
Corn would sing lead, Bean & Squash do

                the doo-wahs & scat

          tortillas
          hushpuppies
          grits
          succotash

corn liquor—white

        lightning silage/ seepage

                & a chorus line of dead
                drunk cows.

Any

     echt-

           American eclogue would be inescapably involved
tinged with corn—let's call it High Corn—
like Harry Smith's collection of old 78's—
thin eerie corniness of the Carter Family
like angels with pellagra

             or North Mexican radio polkas
w/ Bavarian tubas & Charro guitars

                musical offerings
to a sacred kachina cornmeal painting by

             Norman Rockwell
or Spoonbread American Eleusinian Hoe-Down
pastoral corn

       blue grass
       Celto-Appalachian
       blues for

                        white people
grand guignol border minstrelsy
Child ballad gothic crossed with West African
                                syncopated banjo
no morbid sentimentality or baptist angst
can wither the throbbing orgone
                        of this cornpone.

Aunt J____ from Jessup used to say
apropos Willy Nelson: country music is the true
American poetry
                and wasn't there weeping on
                                muddy graves
                in thunder storms
too much whiskey—suicide—brother-in-law
                                in the KKK
                        State Prison land adjoined
                                their farm
                        & once an escaped murderer
                        was found by bloodhounds in
                                                their
barn
cocktails & gambling on fighting cocks
                                down on the Eastern Shore
her husband Uncle A_____ was a genius of corn
grew the best Silver Queen sweet white
                                ever tasted
cooked Thanksgiving turkey w/ squirrels in
                                cornmeal pepper crust
w/ blue ribbon corn relish/piccalilli recipe
handed down from his grandmother—he hunted
                                —he fished—
& he was out of his fucking mind.

                                                  Music
to keep driving all night by on coffee & bennies
till dawn finds you three states away
on fading radio stations nothing but
                                    gospel or C & W
adverts for hog feed & patent medicine
sermons & miles & miles of
                              hybrid corn.
Big Combines are taking over
                            foreclosing on mortgages
corn is assuming its Spectral aspect
                                    —revenge of the Corn Goddess
—mad cow disease—frankenfoods—autism—
cornflakes originally invented as
cure for masturbation now cause childhood obesity
—Ritalin—halfdead midwestern farm towns
grain silos rusting beside orphan
                              railway tracks
Evil Corn
            Anti-Pastoral Corn
                                    denatured corn
no spirit no taste
                        ghost husks of
                                    post-modern corn
toxic blandness—
                  you can hear it in the music
like suffocating in a plastic bag—
                              neo-con corn
corn on steroids
                  cornball imperialism
                              let them eat corn.

Demeter weeps for her daughter in Hell
keeps the seed power hidden

                causes a most terrible
                & dog-like year to occur
                        again & again
robs the gods of the greasy smoke of sacrifice
that symbolizes human reciprocity with nature
& resolves the dialectic in a Paracelsan

                     trialectic
that hinges on a single pomegranate seed's
secret psychotropic identity—which according to

                  my old pen-pal the late
                  Dr Mahdihassan of Pakistan whose work
                  is cited in Needham's

                        Sci. & Civ. in China
is the ruby chalice of the lapis philosophorum
hazelnut of the Salmon of Wisdom at the

                    Source of the Boyne
Hesperidean apple

          poisoned apple
              blood drop deep
sacrifice

        gift
            magic bean
                the blight on the corn
                that kills you
is also Gilgamesh's lost herb of immortality

                thunderbolt child born in hell
                like a flash of light from

underground
Iacchos the esoteric Bacchus

          the Pastoral Redeemer

                                        the Mead of Poetry.
Triple Goddess—Persephone

                        Demeter

                                    Hecate

            beans

                        corn

                                squash.

Flux

        morphology

                        Linnaeus dressed as a

                                    Lappish shaman
three crows on a dead branch

                            the Andrews Sisters.
L. Frank Baum was the Midwestern Swedenborg
Emerald City of Hermes Trismegistus
hobo utopia

                    Zephyrs of Cockaigne
a tramp's view of heaven

                        an Irish OZ
hasty pudding houses thatched in bacon

                            bogs of whipped schlag
trees fruiting w/ blackpuddings

                        etc. ad nauseam

                                    or tobacco
                            Offer tobacco
to the Three Sisters—the blue smoke
                    of visible prayer.

(NOTE: See "The Homeric Hymn to Demeter," trans. by Charles Stein; the recipe
for Corn Zephyrs Cockaigne is from *The Joy of Cooking*. Tip-o-the-fez to M. Pollan.)

Negative Capability Eclogue

Pressed all winter beneath a pall of snow
dead weeds & fallen leaves putrefy
till Spring melts & then dries them
into yellow wounds such as you see
when bandages are unwound
—mummified mud

                    that suddenly shivers

like Ardis Bey beneath the pyramid
stirring to hideous life after 3000 years
now sporting a fez

              coagulates & then

                    relaxes into slime

Upstate dairy farm in late February

          attar of decaying snow

              & old wind

heartbroken bouquet of last summer's hay
lake of mire created by creatures

                  with 3 or 4 stomachs each

then frozen in place again—then

          liquefied one last time as

spiteful goodbye of Frost Giants
Winter's Last Will & Testament—parchment
liver-spotted with age & decay—

                  ink scented w/ musk

according to Wang Pi's Commentary on

                  The Changes

snowdrop or fiddlehead unfolding

               natura naturans

Nigredo
pregnant darkness
original Chaos

hieroglyphic monad
cosmic cheese
birth of the bleus
It's corny—yes it's stupid—like
peasants in a Japanese Samurai flick—
Pathetic Fallacy
                    Nature mourns
                              Nature rejoices
Lamarck—Lysenko—no no—it's
                              too horrible
                    Dionysus
                        crucified
                                        in
an art déco style acte gratuit—
                              André Gide in
                              black beret & sunglasses
contemplating the ruined pastoral economy
of French North Africa ...

Speaking as Darwinians
                    (Erasmus that is
                        not Charles)
the Veil of Isis shimmies
                    so nasty & so tasty
Tijuana Circus designed by
                    Gustave Moreau
Little Egypt in the altogether or the
creature from the black&blue lagoon—
                                        who cares
since as Ibn 'Arabi sez the moth
that attains union with the candle
                        brings back no report.
Opera without music.

                                In fact
opera without actors or audience.
A fetish for purdah. Where it all began
as Hesiod says in form-loving mud
                        the play of light on water.

THE ROUT

Questionnaire
the act of treason &/or criminal anarchy I'd most
like to commit would be:
                fill in the blank
use extra paper if necessary:
                the Triumph of Dionysus.
I love a parade or invasion by any
                foreign power—
an Asian minor—the effeminate Bacchus
conqueror of India
                "I am dynamite"
chariot drawn by snakes & leopards
biker transvestite maenads
                ithyphallic fauns
                crowd of naked yokels
                w/ tails & horns
Bassarids, Evantes, Euhyades, Edonides,
Trieterides, Ogygies, Mimallonians,
Thyades & Bacchae w/ serpents round
                their waists
decked out in goatskins stagskins
                thyrsi of pinecones
fillets of vine leaves
                then—Silenus leaning
                on his fennel stalk
tremulous plump potbellied donkey-eared
riding jackass & dressed in drag
                (a shabby yellow gown)
surrounded by naked horned cruel satyrs
with permanent satyriasis
                dancing the rhumba

& Pan the hairythighed with his

Hemipans

Aegipans

Sylvans

Fatui

Lemurs

Lares

Elves &

Hobgoblins   & Priapus

                                                      the talking dick

                                                      the garden gnome

                                                      w/ a dildo

                                  the triumphal chariot

all covered with ivy gathered on Mt Meru

drawn by elephants covered w/ ivy

the whole rout wreathed in ivy

takes over like kudzu on an Alabama farm

sporting trophies standards banners spoils booty

singing triumphal cantos loud dithyrambs

little rustic ditties & Argentinian tangos

                                              from *Martin Fierro*

See *Gargantua & Pantagruel* V/39 − 40

See *Hypnerotomachia Poliphili*

                                  "Triumph of Vertumnus & Pomona"

                                  "Triumph of Priapus"

                                  (censored w/ a smear in

                                  nearly every surviving copy of

                                  this incunabulum)

See Nonnos of Panopolis *Dionysiaca*

                                  passim, e.g. Book XIV

Centaurs

Hyads

Pheres   on brassbacked drums

Nymphs
Oreads

Bassarids
Corybantes
Cyclopians
Rockdwellers   } on wood winds
Sons of Hermes
Dactyloi
Telechines

Tityri
Naiads
Hamadryads
Cabeiroi   cymbals tambourines
Gnomes   woodblocks triangles
Sylphs   (cf. Moondog & Harry Parch)
Salmanders
Undines
And dolphins in aquariums on wheels
& black panthers on silver leashes

& they'd all
march across Connecticut like
                    Sherman thru Georgia
                        cross the Hudson
                            cross the Thru-way
transform a 60-mile-wide swath of Upstate New York
back into pastoral landscape circa 1795
Dutch genre scene w/ cows & watermeadows
Indians forests escaped Maroons &
                        vile heretics
destroying Civilization wherever he passes
the emblematic hieroglyphic victorious procession

of wild-ass Dionysus & his always
drunk always stoned always queer
pagan militia. Circus parade. Shall be
                              utterly transformed.
Into a green thought in a green shade.
                              Philadelphia Mummers Parade.

ORIGIN OF THE VINE

Nonnos lived in PANopolis in Egypt
in the 5th cen. AD—shag-end of the
                              Classical world—
his own editor & translator despise his
decadence—"stale … exhausted … a faded
& overcrowded tapestry moving a little
                              now & then
as the breath of his sickly unwholesome
                              fancy stirs it"
                              (see *Loeb Lib.* ed.)

late & decadent—our favorite flavors—
drooping poppy narcissus in Saharan simoom
languid unrolling of scrolls by Nile-side
under palm tree & crescent moon of
nursery-tale simplicity—
                              EgyptLand—
                                        themepark
of magical curiosa & paederastic pastoral—
                                        gnostic/libertine
mystical love papyrus. Red wine
is the Red Philosopher's stoned & lolling
swish oriental playmate—Ampelos of Lydia
(nowadays part of the Ottoman Empire)
"a new sprout of the Loves—no bloom on chin

146

no down yet marked snowy cheeks
golden flower of youth—curls escaped
over silverglistening shoulders, floated
in whispers disclosing his neck—

                                        unshadowed light
flashed a moon piercing damp cloud from within—
voice of honey silvery foot flowers spring up
eyes turn soft as calf's two moons"
and the Editor warns us "in the
                                     succeeding narrative
Ampelos et al. are ONLY PERSONIFICATIONS
of things connected with vines & drinking"
under no circ's to be taken as fond memories
or onanoneiric fantasies of this all
                             too mauve & tarnished-silver
                                          poet.

Slain while trying to ride a bareback bull Ampelos
is mourned by Dionysus (who otherwise never wept)
till the Fates relent & "a great miracle
is shown to Bacchus as in some Mystery
the lovely dead rose of himself as
                           crawly snake
which turned into a healtrouble flower his belly
now a long long stalk his fingers grew
                           toptendrils
feet took root curlclusters to
                           grape clusters
fawnskin to polybloom'd fruit his long neck
to bunch of grapes elbow bending twig
                       swollen w/ dusk-berries
head's horns spiraling
                     in twisted clumps of drupes
& now rows of plants stretched out

selfmade orchard twining green loops
round trees w/ garlands of unknown fruit"
as if Caravaggio's Eros were to be over-painted
by Arcimboldo into a boy made

> out of grapes

FAY CE QUE
VOULDRAZ
inscribed over the Phalanstery gateway
emblazoned on banners as the

> Oenologico-Viticultural Association

marches with brass band out to harvest like bees

> on heat

in antiquarian orgies of erudite obscurity
worthy of Pantagruel as 'pataphysician

> to the stars—

followed by 23-course gastrosophical pic-nic
with sparkling wines

> a Departure for Cythera

by Boticelli—a banquet with Queen Liberty
on alchemical meats & vintages
steganographic vegetables &

> paracelsan salts

in a Botanic Garden laid out by Erasmus Darwin
for sexcapades with Nature Elementals by
Fuseli & Blake

FIFTH COLUMN
foreign agent spy bund shortwave
radio talkshow spouts violent overthrow
of US Govt. & Xtian morality by
Nietzschean Dionysan eco-terrorists high on
Zarathustrian Haoma & Rastafarian Pantagruelion
Thelemite undercover class traitors &

                        miscegenists
overwhelm & obliterate all traces of the modern world
whole cities melt in surrealist spagyric rays
leaving humans naked beasts bewildered &
wolves in the Catskills. Evoi Iacchos.

                    ET IN ARCADIA EGO
gathering wildflowers to crown our idol
animate it w/ telesic conundrums & yantras
according to the Latin Aesculapius—
                                            give it life
out of our breath & summon it like
the Earl of Bothwell & his coven on the
sea-cliff calling up a great storm to
                                    drown the King
                                        at sea
Dionysus to return again from India
where he's lived all these years incog
under the guise of Shiva on a rampage
of creative destruction
                                    Lord of Misrule
                                            Avatar of Chaos
irrational toxic blind drunk Bacchus
gas-stations & McMansions crumble
in picturesque ruin & vines conquer
the Hudson Valley infrastructure
                                    Destroy
                                        Eradicate
Throw yr high-heeled sabot into the
nauseatingly electromagnetic concrete grid
of dreary materialism & anti-sexual hysteria
like a blotto Wobbly Gargantua.
Breughel. Bakhtin. Bachelard. Bakunin.

Restore the Mysteries
       maenadic lycanthropy & omophagy
              entheogenic orgiastic
                    Harmony.

The signal lamps are lit by night
& the pirate barque lies offshore
its masts wreathed w/ vatic ivy.